# My Beloved,
# My Friend

### The Song of
### Songs for Couples

# My Beloved, My Friend

## The Song of Songs for Couples

Brent D. Christianson

JUDSON PRESS
PUBLISHERS SINCE 1824

Join our mailing list for updates and special offers.
www.judsonpress.com/mailing_list.cfm

Interior design by Beth Oberholtzer.
Cover design by Wendy Ronga and Hampton Design Group.


**Library of Congress Cataloging-in-Publication Data**

Names: Christianson, Brent D., author.
Title: My beloved, my friend : the Song of Songs for couples / Brent D.
    Christianson.
Description: 1st [edition]. | Valley Forge : Judson Press, 2017.
Identifiers: LCCN 2016031974 (print) | LCCN 2016045516 (ebook) | ISBN
    9780817017767 (pbk. : alk. paper) | ISBN 9780817081669 (e-book)
Subjects: LCSH: Man-woman relationships—Biblical teaching. | Bible. Song
    of Solomon—Criticism, interpretation, etc. | Married people—Prayers and
    devotions.
Classification: LCC BS1485.6.M25 C47 2017 (print) | LCC BS1485.6.M25
    (ebook) | DDC 223/.906—dc23
LC record available at https://lccn.loc.gov/2016031974

Printed in the U.S.A.

First printing, 2017.

# CONTENTS

Most of us fall in love. Many of us find that love leading us into a life commitment to the one we love. Sometimes those relationships end and there is a lot of pain. Even when those commitments deepen and endure, the inevitable challenges and hard work of making the relationship last are just as enduring. Of course, there is a lot of pleasure, a lot of joy, a lot of happiness, and a lot of fun as well! Those of us who have both fallen in love and joined our lives to another's life know that.

Thank God, as many of us know, even the challenges of something we consider worthwhile can be constructive. I wrote this booklet as a married person for people who are dedicated to sharing their lives with each other. I celebrate with you the joy that such relationships give. I understand that because we are human we can challenge each other. And I know, as you know, that because it takes work to build anything, it takes work to build a loving life together. I offer this book as a tool for your use.

These meditations are inspired by the beautiful and often neglected book from the Hebrew Bible, the Song of Songs (or, the Song of Solomon). Each meditation begins with selected verses from the book, followed by a short reflection. After each reflection are a number of activities or discussion questions for you to try as a couple. Choose from among them, or use an activity you devise for yourselves. A poem ends each meditation. Unless otherwise indicated, I am the poet—and my advice for poetry in general is that you don't look for what a poem means, but what it *does* to you—how it makes you *respond* or *feel,* much like a loving relationship.

Include prayer as a part of your time together. Many couples find it difficult to pray together, so begin with one-sentence prayers and try moving on from there. You may wish to use the prayers provided for each meditation. I have more to say about ways you can use this book in the following pages.

Most of us fall in love. The two of you, like my beloved and friend, Rebecca, and I, and millions of others, have chosen to commit and remain together. Let's have fun while we work to build relationships of strength and beauty.

Brent D. Christianson
Madison, Wisconsin

# HOW TO USE THIS BOOK

Talk; listen; respond; ask questions; give answers; have fun. Okay, that isn't very specific, is it? There are twenty-six meditations in this book and one preliminary exercise (reading the Song of Songs together). Depending on your situation, you may easily be able to find a half hour to an hour for yourselves to read and discuss. If there are family members, children, or time constraints, you will have more difficulty; but I urge you to set aside time.

You may be tempted to go through one meditation a day. I don't recommend that. Try no more than two a *week* (unless you're in a retreat setting). Take turns reading each meditation. Read the suggested discussion topics or exercises and agree on which you want to try. You may want to give yourselves time to think about your answers for some of the questions (overnight or in the course of the day if you read the meditation in the morning). With six discussions or activities in each meditation, you may want to choose just one and return to the meditation at a later date to try another option.

You will have space in the margins to take notes or make observations; use the space.

You may want to plan a personal couple retreat for an overnight or a weekend. That would be a good idea. Choose two of the topics for each day you are away. Spend time in reading, discussion, contemplation, and . . . relaxation!

The primary intent of this book is not so much to "rescue" relationships in trouble, but to strengthen relationships in which both partners want to improve how they live and how they love. My experience, not only as a pastor for thirty-six years but as part of a couple for forty years, is that we don't take enough time to talk and listen. My hope is that this book will give you opportunity for quality, compassionate, and loving time together.

# GETTING STARTED
## THE SONG OF SONGS

The Song of Songs isn't one of the best-known books of the Bible. That's a pity, because it is a delightful celebration of the joy of love—not just love as an ideal, but the real, wonderful, confusing, and sometimes scary love that two people share. The book is sensual and erotic. The term *erotic* has taken on meanings for us that aren't necessarily true to its original meaning. To be erotic is "to long." Longing can be holy. We meet a God in the Bible who longs for the human creature and for all creation. Our longing for each other can reflect that love.

We are physical. God intended that. We express our longing and our love in physical ways. God intended that too. We celebrate love and longing in many ways. The Song of Songs is an example of one of those ways.

Fundamentally, the Song of Songs is a poem. Poetry is a different kind of language that speaks in pictures and impressions and descriptions. It can pass through time and emerge looking still new and splendid, as much of this biblical book has done.

But it also can carry with it language and images that might not make as much sense in a different time or culture. For example, for me to tell my wife her hair is "like a flock of goats" (6:4) might not be well-received. Other words, however, still connect with us. Can't we feel the emotions these words bear: "Upon my bed at night I sought him whom my soul loves; I sought him, but found him not; I called him, but he gave no answer" (5:3)?

During the Middle Ages, monks—who lived single and celibate (they didn't marry)—wrote more commentaries on the Song of Songs than on any other book in the Older Testament. The usual Christian interpretation in that time held that the book is an allegory that describes the relationship of Jesus and the church.

I think the monks knew what it was really about and enjoyed reading it for what it was!

Much of the Song of Songs comes from very ancient love poetry. The Song of Songs took its present form more than 300 years before Jesus was born. It is a gift from that time to all times. Enjoy it.

• • •

Before you begin the meditations in this volume, take time to read the Song of Songs together. Read it aloud. The main characters in the book are the lovers (male and female in the book), their friends, their family, and the "daughters of Jerusalem." You choose which voices you want to be; it helps to have each of you stay "in voice" for each reading, but it will be fun to switch roles too.

When you have read it together at least once, talk about these things:

1. What parts did you enjoy the most?
2. What parts seemed strange?
3. What moved you the most?
4. And, because it is a poem, don't talk about what it means, but what it does. What is its effect and impact on you?

# The ONE I Love

*As a lily among brambles*
  *so is my love among maidens.*
*As an apple tree among the trees of the wood,*
  *so is my beloved among young men.*
  —Song of Songs 2:2-3

Do you remember the first very special gift you ever received? I got a Davy Crockett Coonskin Cap when I was four years old and in the hospital. My Aunt Esther gave it to me. I knew that every third boy in my town had one, but this hat was different. It was special; it carried with it the love of an aunt, the memory of a healing, and the presence of love.

Do you remember what it was like to find each other? It could be that the first time you saw each other, something happened and you *knew* this was the *one*. But, chances are you really don't remember the first time you saw each other. What you might remember is the first time the *one* began to be different from the *others*.

There are a lot of people in the world! But somehow the two of you found something special in each other. Somehow you were drawn to each other. When you decided this was more than magnetism, you looked for and found in each other one who is special for you.

Love—the long-lasting kind—causes us to see the other as special, extraordinary, unlike others. We see that not because the other is perfect (now, stop laughing!), but because we have found and continue to find things in each other that are unique and special and good.

We may be the only ones to see that uniqueness, that specialness, that goodness. That's okay; we're the only ones who need to see it. Seeing it is only part of the gift. We don't always continue to tell each other what we see. The saying and the hearing make the gift more real and more alive and more a part of our present—and more a part of our future.

### Some Things to Talk About

1. A lily among thorns? An apple tree among common wood? Have some fun and think of images from the world you would use to describe each other.
2. Think of the things you saw in each other that attracted you when you first met. Share them.
3. Think of the positive things that you have seen in each other since you met that you didn't know were there before. Share them.

### Some Things to Do

1. Make an apple pie and set it by a bouquet of lilies. Breathe in the fragrance of the flowers and share a slice of pie as you celebrate the unique qualities you love in the other.
2. Is there a song that you consider "yours"? Play it or sing it together.
3. Finish this phrase: "You are special to me because. . . ."

**Prayer**

Dear God, in this world of great variety we thank you. We thank you for the beauty of the earth, rich with many things. We also thank you that in this vast world you have led us to each other. Help us to treasure the uniqueness we find in each other. Help us to grow as individuals and as a couple. Help us to love you and to love each other. For Christ's sake. Amen.

# I Thought of You Today

Remembering you in our canoe,
    the green of the forest,
      the blue of the lake,
        the gold of your hair,
          the turquoise and cotton sky.
You are strong and beautiful
as you paddle
with rhythms of wood and wave
    and ponder
    the fluid vagaries
    of life.
You see with eyes,
    clear and blue.
You move
    with grace received and nourished,
bringing our canoe to the portage,
walking our lives through this trail.
      I thought of you today;
    you, my path
   between
moment and mystery.

# Made for Longing and Desire

*Upon my bed at night*
*I sought him whom my soul loves;*
*I sought him, but found him not;*
*I called him, but he gave no answer.*
*When I found him whom my soul loves,*
*I held him and would not let him go. . . .*
*. . . I am my beloved's,*
*and his desire is for me.*
　—Song of Songs 3:1,4 (adapted); 7:10

What are some of the things you really, *really* wanted as a child? A certain kind of bike or book, outfit or instrument, toy or privilege? We learn early on what it means to long for something, to desire something. In fact, as humans we are probably born with the ability to long and desire. An infant can be very insistent longing for a 2 a.m. feeding.

We soon find that we are changed and shaped by the things we long for.

The thing we long for may prove to be more our master than our servant. Longing for something as though it could save us turns us into worshipers of a false god. Addictions are longings bent and expanded out of shape and proportion. Some longings are silly—a victory for our team, a car we neither need nor can afford, winning the lottery.

Then someone comes along—that one with whom we share life—and longing and desire take on a different meaning. The lovers in the Song of Songs long for each other. And that longing changes them. They can no longer be persons for themselves, but are also persons for each other. They desire to be together; they desire to love and make love; they desire simply to know the other desires them.

Such intense longing fades, sooner or later. It fades, but it does not disappear. We grow into each other. We find pleasure and purpose and comfort and completion and joy in each other. When we are apart, we long for each other and desire to be with the other.

In our longing, we see the image of God in ourselves. God longs for us. Your longing for each other, rather than being sordid or naughty, is, in fact, contact with your own God-touched humanity.

### Some Things to Talk About

1. Tell each other about a time you were apart and the longing to be together was intense.
2. Tell each other about something you really, *really* wanted when you were young.
3. Think of three ways that your longing for each other has changed you. Share them.

## Some Things to Do

1. Find a poem or a song that expresses longing and desire as you experience it. Share it.
2. Write a poem for your partner that expresses longing, desire, and love.
3. Rent or go to a movie about two people who long for each other. Watch it and hold hands.

## Prayer

God, you long to be with us. Your desire is to be loved by your world. Your longing is strong enough to bring you to us forever. When we realize that, we feel a deeper sense of relationship to you because we know how strong our longing is for each other. We know how we desire each other. We see how our longing is profound and wonderful. Thank you for wanting us. Thank you for helping us to want each other. In Christ. Amen.

# Preparations

Cooking for you . . .
the recipe in a book
or in my mind so when
I close my eyes to think
of what it might be,
    I see your face.
Finding the right pots and pans,
    like making the bed just right,
not to keep it made but because
    the unmaking is so delightful.

The oil heats
    or is warmed for massage. . . .
Chopping herbs and greens and spices,
their scents change as they are touched—
    like you, like me.
The sound of frying,
the smell of fresh bread,
    the scent of candles on the table,
    next to the bed,
the moment when we close our eyes,
breathe in, pray.

Then lovely, lovely meeting of
    what is prepared
    and we,
    who are prepared.

# When You're Alone

*My beloved has gone down to his garden,*
*to the bed of spices,*
*to pasture his flock in the gardens,*
*and to gather lilies.*
  —Song of Songs 6:2

When you were a child, did you have a favorite space or place where you could be alone—to read, to play, to rest, to think? When our grandson, Silas, stays with us, sometimes he has demands on our space and time to play one board game or another, to read with him, to play catch. But sometimes he just wants to be alone, constructing wonders out of wooden blocks, reading a book, or playing a game by himself.

As a boy, I enjoyed hiking alone in the woods of Wisconsin, playing guitar in my bedroom, or hiding in the space in the lilac bushes between our yard and the house next door. I wasn't a loner, but in a family of nine children, it was good to have some alone time.

Children have a natural instinct (often, but not always!) for what it is that they may need—a hug, a word of assurance during a storm, or some good old alone time.

When the two of you made a commitment to be life partners, you promised to be together until death finally parts you.

That is a major commitment, perhaps the greatest a person can make. But you didn't promise that you would be joined at the hip with no chance to be separate or alone. Even individuals in the most intimate and committed of relationships need alone time.

Dietrich Bonhoeffer, the German pastor and martyr, writing for members of the Confessing Church living in community, cautioned that whoever cannot be alone will have trouble living in community, and whoever cannot live in community will have trouble being alone. Both solitude and fellowship are needed in all communities; both are needed in the lifelong commitment you have made to each other.

Why take time to be alone? For lots of good reasons: time to rest and be quiet (a precious commodity in our "wired" world); time to work on a hobby or project; time to think, to pray, to meditate; time to be "in your garden"—whether that is a real flower or vegetable garden or just a metaphor for becoming reacquainted with the earth—to tend and be attentive. Being alone, when it is your conscious choice, also makes being together much healthier and more fulfilling.

What is your preferred rhythm, as individuals and as a couple? Do you prefer spontaneity? ("Hey, could I have Saturday morning to myself? I need some time to work on my weaving.") Or do you prefer advanced planning? ("How about every third Sunday we plan on taking time for ourselves from noon until 8:00?") You are probably some mixture of the two.

But time alone should be part of your life together. It is not a way of saying, "I need to get away from you," but a chance to be refreshed in your own mind and spirit. You will be refreshed and ready for yourself and ready for each other.

## Some Things to Talk About

1. Did you have a special "alone" place or places when you were a child? If so, describe that for each other.
2. Being alone is not always a positive experience. Think about a time when you were alone and it didn't feel good. Share that experience with each other. What resolved that stress? Share that.
3. How have you made "alone time" a part of your life together, if at all? Discuss how that has worked for you and, if necessary, make changes.

## Some Things to Do

1. If alone time hasn't been part of your life pattern but you would like to include it, each of you make a plan for time for solitude.
2. Go for a walk in a wilderness area near you—a park, the woods, a field. Go together, but take time as individuals also, wandering off for a solitary ramble or sitting alone to think or read.
3. Next time you have alone time, write a poem for your partner that begins with the line "When I think of you. . . ."

## Prayer

God of this magnificent creation, thank you for time and space and place to be together with each other and with others we love. Thank you also for time and space and place to be alone, to breathe in the air and relax. Thank you for ordering a Sabbath and for finding us there. Bless our alone times with your whisper of grace and blessing. In Jesus' name. Amen.

# Calm

The lake is still this morning.
    No waves crash against the stones,
        Quiet clouds above the calm.

        As much variety in stillness
    As in stormy chaos,
Morning sees the complexity of calm.

The young poplar out front
    Moves as little as a painting,
        Its ten thousand textures calm.

        A lone seagull drifts over the bay,
    Not searching for food
But enjoying early calm.

Cloud ribbons over the water
    Wrap the morning as a gift,
        Holding the present, pleasant, calm.

        You watch the trillion ripples,
    See the tiny bright line on the horizon,
Think of your life, and love the calm.

# When You're Together

*Come with me from Lebanon, my bride;*
  *come with me from Lebanon.*
*Depart from the peak of Amana,*
  *from the peak of Senir and Hermon,*
*from the dens of lions,*
  *from the mountains of leopards.*
  —Song of Songs 4:8

The commitment the two of you have made is that you will be together "for better or for worse, through sickness and through health, for richer or poorer"—in whichever way you phrased your promise. That promise holds you lovingly accountable to each other.

The thing is, and you probably know this, simply "being together" is not sufficient for living out your promise. What you do when you're together is the necessary element that will make your life together richer and satisfying.

So, what can you do when you're together?

Well, sometimes nothing . . . but only sometimes. When the day or the week has been tiring, when coming up with something to do seems to be another thankless task, then it is good simply to sit, put on your favorite music, or watch a movie, something passive or at least relaxing.

But more often you will want to have something—*some-thing*—on your plates. The poet Donald Hall, writing of his life with Jane Kenyon, mentions what he calls the "third things." That is, the tasks they would undertake together like house-cleaning, visiting homebound people, and yardwork. Those kinds of daily chores had the value of the two of them focusing on one thing and in the course of that one thing, sensing the bond between them growing. Think about those daily/weekly/seasonal activities you share. Make them intentional and pur-posefully relational.

Take time to talk to each other. Most couples don't do that enough. Use vocabulary, expressions, and body language to communicate and increase your comfort with communication and with each other. "Third things" are fine, but I recommend giving yourselves time each day when you're not watching tele-vision, washing dishes, eating meals, or driving somewhere to look into each other's eyes and talk. Take at least a minute each day to tell each other something good about your day, or some-thing that wasn't so good—or both.

Plan a trip and take it. The lover in Song of Songs invites the beloved to leave the wilds of Lebanon, the forests and the beasts, and to take time together to look from mountains, to experience something different but together. These things don't have to cost an arm and a leg; a day trip here or there can be as rewarding as a two-week getaway on a cruise ship—if you take the time to talk to each other about what you see.

Being together doesn't automatically give you a better rela-tionship, but being intentional about that time certainly will.

### Some Things to Talk About

1. What are the "third things" that you do together? Talk about how you feel when you are involved in them.
2. Share a time you spent together that was good. Tell each other what made it good.
3. Set aside a specific period of time each day to be together without distractions. Share what was good about your day and something you appreciate about each other.

### Some Things to Do

1. Lie on the grass, hold hands, and share what you see in the cloud shapes.
2. Get up early and watch the sunrise together. Then watch the sunset together that evening. Write a poem comparing your lover to a sunrise and a sunset.
3. Plan a new "third thing" and set a specific time to try it.

### Prayer

God, you have said that it is not good for a person to be alone and out of a close relationship. You yourself have chosen to be together with a whole creation. Thank you for bringing us together. Thank you for giving us time together. Give us love and grace to make our time together a joyful blessing. In Jesus' name. Amen.

# Book Ends

Remember reading *Wind in the Willows*,
a chapter at a time, to each other
before we allowed ourselves to fall asleep?
Remember uproarious laughter at Mr. Toad
when he first saw a motor car,
how long it took us to catch our breath?
Remember bringing books with us
to read in the quiet after a day of paddling,
flashlights at night, sunlight on rest days?
Remember those times one of us looked up
from the book we were reading and shared
a few sentences we liked and knew the other would like?
Remember the days spent while you read
*Harry Potter*, sometimes sharing with Leah
and I tiptoed out of the way?
Remember, as we begin to sift through our books
and narrow down what will stay as more than memory
that we won't know for a long time how this book ends.

# You Gotta Have Friends

*We will exult and rejoice in you;*
  *we will extol your love more than wine;*
  *rightly do they love you.*
  —Song of Songs 1:4b

Who were your first friends? Did you meet in the sandbox in kindergarten? Did they move in next door and become new playmates? Did you see each other in church, in Scouts, in sports, or in school? We each need friends. Friends help us to be who we are.

Throughout the Song of Songs, friends of the couple offer their views on the relationship, ask questions of one or the other, give advice to them, and even describe some of the action. Sometimes they clarify the situation. Sometimes they allow the lover or beloved to clarify the relationship. Often they just sit there and listen like good friends.

God created us to live in community. Your relationship is a part of that intention in creation. As individuals and as a couple, you have friends as a part of living out that intention of God. Chances are pretty good that when you were dating, each of you had friends who offered running commentaries on your relationship. Each of you had friends to whom *you* offered running commentaries on your love. Each of you have friends now who share in your life, whether by offering advice or, more wisely, by sitting and listening.

Each of you is also a friend. You are a friend to your friends, of course. But you also are a friend to each other. Lovers who don't become friends soon cease being lovers. You become friends with each other in the same way you became friends with others. You share together, you offer advice to each other, you receive advice from each other, you laugh together, you cry together, and sometimes you just sit and listen.

Your friendship is more than just a part of God's creation. You reflect the God who chooses to be your Friend in your time together. You see each other as God sees you—as unique, as beautiful, as awesome, and as friends.

### Some Things to Talk About

1. Who were your best friends in childhood (from preschool on up)? Tell each other about them.
2. Who are your friends now? Describe to your partner who you think his or her friends are. Listen and clarify.
3. What elements that you look for in a friend do you find in each other?

### Some Things to Do

1. Tell each other jokes—even bad ones!
2. Invite friends you enjoy over for an evening.
3. Volunteer in a place that asks you to befriend someone else, whether mentoring a young person, helping out at a senior center, or visiting people who are hospitalized or homebound.

**Prayer**

Dear God, you have befriended the whole world. We thank you for that. We thank you also for the friends you have given us all through our lives. Thank you for those friends who ran with us through school, those friends who walked with us through our adult years, and those friends who are dear to us now. We thank you especially that you have helped us to be friends to each other. Bless this friendship, dear Friend of all. Amen.

# Cedar Avenue

Right here . . . this intersection,
not far from where our friend
saw Marlon Brando and two
AIM activists.
Right here . . . this intersection,
near the art shops and the store
where we bought a vase from China,
amazed that we could do that . . .
Right here . . . this intersection,
walking with you, stepping off the curb,
not paying attention to the traffic,
but to you.
Right here . . . this intersection,
life changed when you touched my arm
and called me "honey" for the first time,
right here.

# Time for Seasons

*Look, winter is over,*
*the rains are done,*
*wildflowers spring up in the fields.*
*Now is the time of the nightingale.*
*In every meadow you hear*
*the song of the turtledove.*
*The fig tree has sweetened*
*its new green fruit*
*and the young budded vines smell spicy.*
*Hurry, my love, my friend*
*come away.*
   —Song of Songs 2:11-13, Bloch

Sometimes we experience life as a relatively straight line. Things begin, they move, and they end. But we also experience the way life can run in cycles. Well, washing machines do that, I suppose, but there are also rhythms to life. The moon goes through its phases. We who live where there are four real seasons see each year move through seasonal rhythms.

Each season has its own feel, its own history in our lives, its high points and holidays, expectations and anticipations, dreads and deadlines, smells, tastes, and on and on. We don't all agree on these seasons. I don't care for March; it is one of my coworkers' favorite months.

When we have been in a relationship long enough (and who knows how long "long enough" is!), we have been able to experience the flow of the year and the years, with their sense of movement and return, the holidays, vacations, plantings, harvestings, summer games, winter games, and what those things mean to us and to our relationship.

Our relationships also can have a "seasonal" feel. These may not be as regular as the equinoxes and solstices, but they are there. We might be in an early spring—thawing, a little messy, but with a sense of anticipation. We might be experiencing a relational summer—long hot days, clear nights, the song of birds, and the smell of flower gardens. We might be having a wintry time—experiencing chilly to frigid conditions, relying on lots of layers and external heat sources, or perhaps clinging to each other for warmth while the snowy blast rattles life's window.

For the lovers in the Song of Songs, the rich promise of spring matched their anticipation and their sense of future and hope that made their "now" exciting and beautiful. We are able to use our (common) sense and our senses to take in the reality of the world around us; we can use those same things to shape and understand the realities of the world that is our relationship with one we love.

### Some Things to Talk About

1. What are your favorite seasons? Describe them and why you enjoy them.
2. Share with each other the smells you associate with each time of year. Why are those scents significant?
3. Describe your current relationship as a season—what is that season and why do you identify your relationship as such?

### Some Things to Do

1. Go for a walk or a drive in the country, taking time to notice the sights, sounds, and smells of the season.
2. What season is it now (winter, spring, summer, fall)? Plan an activity to do together that fits the season and weather.
3. Listen to Vivaldi's "The Four Seasons." Enjoy the contrasting movements and how they express the turning cycles of the year—in creation and in life.

### Prayer

God of the turning seasons, thank you not only for giving us a world of beauty and variety, but also for bringing us together to experience life in such a world. Open us to the world and the community where we live. Open us also to each other and help us to see the flow of life, the changes and our own seasons, as gifts from you. In Jesus' name. Amen.

## Love in the Fall

Summer is gone but sometimes
the days are August hot.
A week later the sky looks like snow.
The tomato plant opens
a yellow blossom
that will never turn red.
In the morning you wake
and it is still dark,
extended luxurious nights.
Remember the young lovers
you see in old photos?
They lived past the first frost.
Windows closed at night
open in bright morning
and let in brazen freshness.
Summer is over,
winter has not begun.
The autumn is good.

# A Moving Relationship

*Again, O Shulamite,*
*dance again,*
*that we may watch you dancing!*
*Why do you gaze at the Shulamite*
*as she whirls*
*down the rows of dancers?*
  —Song of Songs 7:1, Bloch

We learn a number of things about the woman in Song of Songs. Among them we read that she is quite a dancer! In this verse her friends comment on her dancing. In the verses that follow, the lover comments in greater detail about the gracefulness of her steps and the natural beauty that her dancing reveals.

In my relationship with Rebecca, it took more than two decades of marriage for me to agree to take dance lessons and discover that, contrary to what I had feared, people didn't watch me on the dance floor like these people watched the Shulamite. But the message I learned and the message here is that such activity is not a way to show off, but a way to show enjoyment of another.

You may dance. And if you do, you may dance well or poorly or somewhere in between. But the lessons of dancing apply to

23

the reality of relationships. When one dances, there is concentration both on something outside oneself—the music—and on something inside oneself—a sense of rhythm and power and grace and movement. When two people dance, at least two additional things happen: concentration not just on the music but on the other, and a sense not only of your movement, but of your feelings for your partner.

Beyond the simple *pleasure* of dancing, a dance is *participation* in the movement and flow of life all around us. The music in nature and the nature of music call us to celebrate being part of a creation where relationships move, the world flows, and we are given the gift of participation in all of that.

I encourage people to dance—it really is fun. But a loving relationship sealed in commitment is itself a dance. You pay attention to the outside world, to your place in its contexts. You pay attention to your inner attitudes and your feelings for the other. Sometimes life is a swing, sometimes a waltz, a polka, a meringue, a rumba, a twist, or movement that you just make up. But if life is life and if relationship is real, it is always moving—internally and externally.

### Some Things to Talk About

1. Not many of us are Fred Astaire and Ginger Rogers in dance or relationship, but each person's strengths may balance the other person's flaws. Share the strengths you see in each other that have helped with your own challenges.
2. Describe a time you watched your partner doing something and found it moving.
3. Share something you see in the world's dance—its life and rhythm—that you appreciate.

**Some Things to Do**

1. Do you dance? Go to a restaurant, club, or somewhere else where you can dance together.
2. Go to a local dance performance—whether it's folk dancers, high school drill team, polka club, or ballet. You'll be able to find something.
3. During a rainy day, find a movie about dancing and watch it together. (Many movie musicals have lots of dancing, such as *A Chorus Line, Hairspray, Kiss Me Kate,* or *An American in Paris.* Other movies feature dancing as part of their story lines, including *Shall We Dance?, Footloose, Billy Elliot, Center Stage,* and *Save the Last Dance.*) Talk about which characters you liked the most.

**Prayer**

God of movement, grace, and love, thank you for the dances around and within us—the flow of life, the music of nature and the music we create, the steps we take in dance and in daily life. Thank you for this partner of mine; help us to love each other and move through life in grace and cooperation. In your name. Amen.

# Smooth
*after Carlos Santana*[1]

Right hand around you,
left hand holding your hand,
the music begins.

Guitar doesn't shriek
but exhales exultation
as the low voice begins.

We move together,
feet forward and backward,
sideways, swaying

Saying, "My Minnesota
Mona Lisa, you are the groove
in my step.

Let's don't forget about it."

**Note**

1. Carlos Santana is a Mexican American musician who became famous for pioneering a fusion of rock and Latin American music, featuring melodic, blues-based guitar lines set against Latin and African rhythms. The final stanza of my poem is an allusion to one of Santana's most popular recordings, "Smooth," from his 1999 album, *Supernatural*.

# Work

*Tell me, my only love,*
*where do you pasture your sheep,*
*where will you let them rest*
*in the heat of the noon?*
*Why should I lose my way among the flocks*
*of your companions?*
  —Song of Songs 1:7, Bloch

How many "jobs" have you had? Do you remember your first job, your best job, your worst job? Do you remember your coworkers, your bosses, your tasks, your pay scale, your schedules? Whew . . . lots of things go into our "jobs."

In the tradition we receive from Scripture, jobs are seen as more than ways to pay for our vacations and more than simple tasks. We use the term *vocation*, which means "calling." And, if there is a calling, there is a caller. God is that caller; and God uses the world, other people, your friends, and your families to do that calling.

A vocation is more than a job—it is the way you serve the world and serve God.

When I work with couples who are preparing to make their commitment public, I tell them that such a commitment will always involve work. It may be that I'm not very romantic

(I *think* I am!), but it is simply true that any calling, any vocation, anything worthwhile involves work.

Your relationship is a calling from God. In this vocation you are called to serve each other, you are called to serve God, and you are called to find meaning and significance in your lives. The "work" in a relationship could mean the daily tasks (and they *are* important)—cleaning, cooking, raking, laundry, paying bills, making plans. It also involves the work that makes your relationship stronger—honesty, openness, vulnerability, forgiveness, knowing that you'll never know everything about each other. That vocation, that calling, makes your relationship not just special, but holy.

### Some Things to Talk About

1. Tell each other about your first jobs, your worst jobs, your favorite jobs.
2. Are you "working" now? Tell each other what you enjoy and what you find unpleasant about your work.
3. In the vocation that is your relationship work, what are the easiest tasks and what are the most challenging tasks? Why?

### Some Things to Do

1. If you discussed "Some Things to Talk About" number 3, note the challenging tasks. Brainstorm ways to grow stronger in accomplishing them, and agree on one thing to try.
2. If possible, arrange a "take your spouse to work" day.
3. If you know a couple whose "work" together you admire, arrange to meet with them and share your respect by giving them a compliment.

**Prayer**

Dear God, you have created a world that needs to have a lot happening for it to work. And it works! Thank you for your care in and for this world. Thank you for calling us into our various tasks. Help us to see that, in doing those things, we serve you and each other. Give us grace and strength to do the work in our relationship that will make us more loving, and more beloved. Amen.

# When You Touch Me

When you touch me
I am a pond and there are ripples
that spread from your fingertips
to the center and deepest part.
When you touch me
I am clay to be molded by you
and always bear your fingerprints,
the marks of your palms and knuckles,
the contours of your art.
When you touch me
I am the air that flows around you
and I feel your pressure and
my pressure making a breeze that
cools and drives us both.
When you touch me
I am myself and you are my life
and I am the place where your touch
and my touch create a world
where we find each other.

# Play

*Take me by the hand, let us run together!*
*My lover, my king, has brought me into his chambers.*
*We will laugh, you and I, and count*
*each kiss,*
*better than wine.*
  —Song of Songs 1:4, Bloch

"All work and no play. . . ." You know the rhyme. Play is built into the fabric of creation. *National Geographic* once published an article about play in the animal world. One series of pictures showed a polar bear approaching a tied-up dog. Rather than the dog running or the bear eating, the dog took a posture of play, and the bear responded with a similar posture. After the proper ritual, the dog and the bear played together for several minutes.

If dogs and bears can use play, friends and lovers sure can!

Some people can be playful in their conversation, in their daily tasks, in their normal interaction. Some people participate in sports and games—bike riding, kickball, softball, volleyball, soccer, card games, board games. Some like spectator sports—a beer and brat under the glorious sun in the left field bleachers, huge foam fingers and football on a brisk October day, the pomp and circumstance and human interest of the Olympics. Some are playful by surprising the other with a gift, an evening out, a weekend somewhere else than where you expected to be. We need sometimes (and maybe more often!) to be silly; we need to not take ourselves so seriously; we need to have fun.

Those who experience satisfaction in their relational commitments have a variety of ways to play, a number of avenues for relaxation, an openness to silliness. How about you? How do you play?

## Some Things to Talk About

1. Tell each other about the games you liked to play as children.
2. Would you like to participate in a recreational activity together? Do some research and find one to try.
3. Tell each other about an activity you haven't done yet but that you think might be fun.

## Some Things to Do

1. If you participate in a sport or other activity together, plan a get-together with your teammates.
2. Go to a park, share a favorite childhood snack (ice cream from the nearby vendor, popcorn, etc.), and watch children play.
3. On a cold or rainy day, make something warm to eat and drink, put on some music, and play a game together.

## Prayer

God, you delight in delight. You have created us to have a sense of the need for play and enjoyment and recreation. Thank you for that gift. Stir that gift up in us. Help us to enjoy enjoyment and each other. In your name. Amen.

## Kick the Can

I am thinking of how we played "kick the can" behind our
  house
in alley cinder that could not cut feet as calloused as ours
and I am thinking of the feel of summer evenings and the
  flock of children
who gathered after supper to choose the game we would
  play
as the sun moved down and cast our growing shadows,
colored kicked-up dust, then set into deepening darkness
while in the lilac bushes in Coney's yard at least one of us
  would hide
while "It" put a foot on the can and counted to a hundred
  and we scuttered
beneath brush, behind sheds, under porches.

I am thinking of summer sounds—locusts and cicadas,
child noises—our voices—as we played, argued, won and
  lost;
dogs barking at our running past their yards, the slamming
  of doors,
the click and fizz when my father opened a can of Peerless
  lager,
the wind through the elms that still spread their branches
  over LaCrosse,[1]
the television in the neighbors' house as they watched "I've
  Got a Secret,"
the radio in the car of the boy picking up neighbor Betty for
  a date,
Pat Boone singing "Speedy Gonzales" and the motor rev-
  ving as they drove away.

I am thinking of thunderstorms echoing through coulees
and the time we saw Mrs. Moser's tree blow over on her
    house;
how streets flooded and we shrieked and splashed, swathed
    in swimming suits
after the storm had passed when our mothers let us out
amid the sound of the chainsaws cutting up the fallen tree.

And I am thinking of the last days of August when we knew
    summer
was wilting and school was starting and we would have new
    books,
clothes, pencils, teachers, new kids and new places in the
    pecking order.
Bronzed maple leaves, the beach and Municipal Swimming
    Pool closed,
we would not go up to Grandma's farm again until Christ-
    mas Eve.
We returned the last of the summer reading books to South
    Branch Library
and shifted our attention from the Braves to the Packers,
knowing that, before summer came again, everything must
    be buried in snow.

**Note**

1. LaCrosse is the name of the town in Wisconsin where I grew up.

# The Beauty of the Beloved

*Ah, you are beautiful, my love;*
 *ah, you are beautiful;*
 *your eyes are doves.*
*Ah, you are beautiful, my beloved,*
 *truly lovely.*
*Our couch is green;*
 *the beams of our house are cedar,*
 *our rafters are pine.*
 —Song of Songs 1:15-17

In his simple "Love Poem," Robert Bly has written that when one is in love, beauty can be found anywhere—the grass, barns, light posts, and even empty streets. Love can help us see beauty everywhere.

Love is exuberant when we are first caught up in it. That feeling of excitement can color the whole world and make things special and beautiful. But as those of us who have been together for more than a few months know, that kind of thrill doesn't last.

That's fine. Part of that thrill is a sort of romantic fog. We don't need to see or know everything right away! Besides, fog has its own beauty. It makes for very lovely sunsets and welcoming mornings.

But as that fog burns away, we are allowed the gift of vision. That vision lets us see with a clarity blessed by God. As our love matures, our eyes take in a world of beauty—beauty that includes someone who sees in me a beauty I can't see, and someone who has a beauty that I can find where others might not be able to.

Look at the words at left from the Song of Songs. The lover is praising the beauty of the beloved in a nearly breathless way. Look at all the *ahhhh*s as the lover stumbles about trying to find the right words.

All of a sudden we run into a description of couches, beams, and rafters! It sounds as though the couple might be in a very nice cabin . . . maybe on vacation.

Or, it sounds as if they have allowed themselves to move carefully, lovingly, eyes wide open, into the clarity of maturing love. The beauty we find in each other may not be the same beauty we saw in each other when we first met, but it is probably much more real, much more certain, and much more beautiful. And that beauty touches all we see—even couches, beams, and rafters.

A wonderful reality of the Hebrew language is that the same word for "beauty" is used to describe both men and women. Beauty is never limited by gender!

You are still together because you each see a beauty in the other that includes but also is deeper than outward appearance. To acknowledge and share your sight and insight increases the beauty in the other and the appreciation in both. Try it.

### Some Things to Talk About

1. What did you find beautiful about each other when you first met?
2. Somewhere, sometime during your relationship you discovered something new and beautiful about each other. Describe to each other what that was, or when it happened.
3. Is your partner like a sunrise, a sunset, an evening, or a day? Think about it and tell each other what and why.

### Some Things to Do

1. Spend time together watching a sunrise, a sunset, an evening, or an early day.
2. If you have the photos and mementos (tickets, programs, and so on), work together on a collage to remind you of your early days.
3. Write an acrostic poem for each other using the word *BEAUTIFUL*. Each letter begins a new line.

### Prayer

God of beauty, you created the universe in a way that makes the word *beautiful* seem hardly enough. Each day we see the beauty of the earth, the sky, the plants, and the animals around us. Each day we are touched by the beauty we find in each other. Open our eyes always to see and to honor that beauty. Thank you for giving us to each other to honor and to love. In Christ. Amen.

## Marta and Thorbjorn

She left Sydnaes farm.
He was born in Eidsvaag.
Norway . . .
In Trump Coulee, Wisconsin, they produced
children, corn, wheat, tobacco, eggs,
and, years after they had died,
looking down from the wall in the hallway,
they produced fear in great-grandchildren
as we tried to sneak
past their framed faces.
I thought they were, like their images,
dismal, severe, pietistic.
When we found a ribboned lock of her hair with
a note expressing her love for him,
her longing for him,
their portraits changed and I heard this song:
"Oh that he would kiss me
with the kisses of his mouth."
O . . . How I Love You.

# Be Proud

*I am black and beautiful,*
*O daughters of Jerusalem,*
*like the tents of Kedar,*
*like the curtains of Solomon.*
—Song of Songs 1:5

Some societies and some religious traditions equate *pride* with arrogance or a failure to sense one's need for God. These are unfortunate traditions. Perhaps you were raised in one of them and taught not only not to think *too* highly of yourself, but not to think highly of yourself at all. Oh, I suppose you could find justification for that in the Bible, but you can just as easily see there is something about the human being that brings forth love in God, which is the central story of Scripture.

There is something about you that your lover saw, sees, and will see. There is something about you that you saw, see, and will see, something that makes pride not only possible but, well, necessary.

The woman in Song of Songs had heard taunting because she is dark-skinned and her labors outside under the hot sun have darkened her complexion even more. Does she look down in shame? Nope. She says, "I am black and beautiful like the tents of the wandering herders . . . shimmering in the sun; I am dark like the expensive curtains in a royal palace." She's not going to let what her society saw as a drawback become something that could hold her back.

Oh, there are all kinds of things that can be used to make us feel shame, many things that prompt the voices that say, "You just don't measure up, do you?" We've all heard them. But there is a stronger voice that says, "Be proud!"

Many stronger voices, really—the voice of God telling you that you are worth God's life; the voice of that life-partner who saw and sees and will see something in you that has made him or her say, "I want to spend my life with that person"; and a voice, maybe deep inside you, saying, "I am beautiful."

Pride is not arrogance; pride is not at anyone else's expense; pride is not dismissive or self-centered or on the attack. Do you as a couple look like the folks in the movies or on TV celebrity shows, or have the blazing influence of whoever is on cable at 4:00 pm? Probably not, but so what? You are pretty darn good at being who you are.

Pride in ourselves allows us to celebrate the pride we find in others—in other couples, in children, in our accomplishments, and in the success of others. Pride is not perfection, but it is persistent in seeing the value of self and others. You have made a commitment to each other—not an easy thing to do, but you've done it. Be proud!

### Some Things to Talk About

1. Make a list of three things about you that make you proud. Share and discuss the lists with each other.
2. Think about how *pride* was thought of in your childhood home, in your community, and in your faith community. Share that and discuss similarities and differences.
3. Something makes you proud of your partner. Tell your partner what and why that is.

**Some Things to Do**

1. Study your community; find an organization that helps people feel proud. Send them a donation or just a note of gratitude.
2. Is there a project, accomplishment, or goal you would both like to achieve that would give you a sense of pride? Name it and make a plan!
3. Is there some aspect of life in your community that works to shame others? If you can agree on what that might be, talk about how to challenge it.

**Prayer** ·

God, you made us. You put in time and effort and love and your own life to craft us. You love us, God and you have given us hearts to love each other. Dear God, help us always to be proud of ourselves and give that pride the grace to help others to love themselves as your precious children. In Jesus' name. Amen.

# With You in the Morning

The coffee is good,
as strong as "I love you,"
as dark as a long kiss.
Steam rises like incense
and blesses the sunrise;
the sun lingers with us.
We drink of the deep warmth
with scent like a new day—
from cups held in silence.

The morning is good.
As new as an old love,
as bright as Earth's greeting.
The fresh snow, a wrapping
for our gifted present
which calls us to linger,
for none know what is waiting
but we know here lying
that life is a blessing.
The evening was good,
as tender as music
and shadowed with kisses.
The blankets enfolded
like guardians of heaven
the gladness we entered.
We slept in the dream world
of daylight's remembrance
and nighttime's glad homing.
With you in the morning,
our hearts beat staccato—
a blues depths of feeling.
I reach out to touch you—
my fingers pay homage,
my eyes see in whispers.
As strong as soft feathers
and tender as granite
we have grown into lovers.

# Be Humble

*I am a wall*
*and my breasts are towers.*
*But for my lover I am*
*a city of peace.*
  —Song of Songs 8:10, Bloch

In the song "Those Seven Deadly Virtues" from the original Broadway production of *Camelot*, the character Mordred (a particularly unpleasant fellow) suggests that the humble don't inherit the earth, but the dirt. And that says in a few words a lot about the way we can misunderstand humility and being humble.

Our society tends to regard "humility" as a good attribute for, well, the really, really humble and not for the achievers, the superstars, the CEOs, and the powerful. We can misread humble as humiliated and not wish that kind of shame on ourselves.

The woman in Song of Songs—in verses we are unlikely ever to hear on a Sunday morning or at a wedding—tells us a great deal about the value and gift of being humble.

She is responding to a teasing by others. As happens so often still, there has been some mockery about physical appearance, maturity, being "grown up," and looking and acting like one is supposed to. Whatever truth the taunt may have had once, it is no longer the case. She has grown and matured, and her strength and beauty are like a mighty walled city. She knows that and can celebrate it. Yet for her lover she is not a fortress, but "a city of peace."

The gift of being humble not only is not the same as humiliation, but it most certainly and strongly refuses to be humiliated. Humiliation comes from the cruelty of others; to be humble is the fruit of a deep internal strength.

I suspect everyone knows what it feels like to be humiliated. Dump that shame. Couples can do that to each other. But couples even more have the gift and the power to make each other strong enough to be humble, self-assured enough not to seek assurance but to give it, proud enough to be humble.

The French have a wonderful phrase for what all of us who are or have ever been young lovers can display: égoïsme à *deux*—self-centeredness as a couple. *Eh bien*, some of that is needed and natural, but as love grows the armor can be dropped and the community formed by the two of you can become a "city of peace."

People who feel under attack will often construct solid walls and fortresses. So in your commitment to each other, live out that peace (which is never lack of conflict, but always space for wholeness and growth). Rejoice in each other for no other reason than the rejoicing itself. Be strong enough to be humble with each other. Paul's words in 1 Corinthians 13 about being gentle, kind, not boastful or arrogant or seeking one's own advantage are not bad guidelines.

You made the most significant step by telling the whole creation (and those witnesses who were with you) that you find enough strength in your love to be humble toward each other and toward the world—being gentle, kind, not out for yourselves, not worried about looking weak, willing not only to hear but to listen, and choosing to be humble people, a city of peace in a world that has too many fortresses.

## Some Things to Talk About

1. Think about someone you thought was truly humble. Talk about that person and what humility looked like in him or her.
2. Make a list of four strengths you see in your relationship. Share those things and discuss how those strengths can help you be humble.
3. If your relationship is fairly new, talk to each other about how being humble will fit into your life together. If your relationship has been around for some years, talk about times you appreciated the humility you saw in your partner.

## Some Things to Do

1. Hey, I don't need to be the only one who defines "humble." Each of you write your own definition and share it. Make an appointment in a week and share how you thought you lived up to that definition in the intervening days.
2. Find a service opportunity in your community where you can be genuinely humble and serving.
3. If the person you thought of in "Some Things to Talk About" number 1 is still living, write a letter (not an e-mail!) expressing how much you appreciated what he or she taught you about being humble, and mail it to that person.

**Prayer**

God, there is no one and nothing anywhere more powerful than you, yet you chose to show yourself in service and humbleness in Jesus. Thank you for such delightful grace. Help us also to be strong enough to be humble. Help us to serve each other, serve our neighbor, and serve our world so that your gift and your example might be real for all. For Christ's sake. Amen.

## Sonnet
*after W.S.*

Shall I compare you to a rising sun?
You have more promise than the start of day
And yet more lovely in your gleaming way
Than the thousand mornings we've begun.
So then, shall I call you my sunset—
The benediction on a day well spent,
The restful beauty of a love that's meant
A life of blessing ever since we met?
No, while the wonder of this glorious earth
Has been a partner in the love we share,
That the glory of each new day's birth,
And sunsets, like the "amen" of a prayer
Are partners to us, doesn't match the worth
Of the life that love has let us share.

# Making Love

*My beloved thrust his hand into the opening,*
*and my inmost being yearned for him.*
*I arose to open to my beloved,*
*and my hands dripped with myrrh,*
*my fingers with liquid myrrh,*
*upon the handles of the bolt.*
—Song of Songs 5:4-5

I have heard that the Inupiat word for making love, when translated into English, is "to laugh." I like that. Because there is something about making love that is funny and fun and more than a little bit strange.

Here is the blessing God has given: God has taken what is, for most living creatures, a means of propagating the species and made it, for humans, a way of losing ourselves in another and then finding a new self there. We misuse God's gift if we treat lovemaking only or even primarily as a way to make babies.

The presence of the Song of Songs in the Scriptures shows that our God and our faith community are *not* against pleasure. We find the joy of sexual pleasure as a gift from God to be shared and celebrated and enhanced and longed for.

Our bodies are put together in such a way—our minds are put together in such a way—that when we make love, the possibility exists for us to meet something deeper than the two of us. We meet the mystery of humankind as God intended it to be—rejoicing in the joy and pleasure we give and receive.

Of course, we who have been together for some time know that not every time is heaven on earth! We know lovemaking can be frustrating and embarrassing and a source of misunderstanding. Don't important things have as great a chance to wound as to make whole?

But joy, as we find it in the Song of Songs, is in the practice, the laughter, the joyful amazement when making love is so good we can't believe it. Joy is in the good humor that allows us to laugh when it could have been better. Joy is that unique and beautiful person with whom we go to bed and with whom we wake up and in whom we can take and give delight.

### Some Things to Talk About

1. Share with each other what you like most about each other's bodies.
2. How is your lovemaking different now than it was when you first made love?
3. When has making love also made you laugh?

### Some Things to Do

1. Do I have to say?
2. Write a poem, draw a picture, or find a poem or work of art that shows what your lovemaking means to you.
3. Plan a way to give yourselves private time away. Take time there to appreciate each other's bodies.

**Prayer**

Dear God, we thank you for our bodies. Thank you for loving this world enough to create. Thank you for loving us enough to create us. Thank you for caring enough to make us sexual creatures. We thank you for the joys, the pleasures, the passion, and the mystery of sex. We thank you for helping us to give ourselves to each other. We ask you to continue to bless our lives and our sexual joy. Help us to rejoice in you and in each other. In Christ. Amen.

# Making Love

Look where the years have brought us!
If we live to be one hundred,
the world will have to grow
to hold our passion.

Each time
the mystery of want and need,
of being drawn and drawing in,
of touching like we've never felt
and feeling like we've never touched—
each time we feel and taste
and move into the garden of delight,
we know
that we do not make love
as much as love makes us.

# What about God?

*All the verses in Song of Songs that mention God:*

_____

_____

_____

_____

Strangely, in this book of the Bible God is never mentioned!

Many of us live in a religious climate that assumes religious people (and politicians) will mention God as often as possible. If God's name isn't used in some way, God is not "there."

Besides, the topics and subjects in the Song of Songs are hardly the kind of "religious" language we are used to, what with all the lust and longing and bodily references! Maybe the book should be modified to get God in there. Or maybe we should do what many commentators have done: claim that this really is a poetic description of God's love for us.

Or just maybe we can be open enough to admit that it is this particular and narrow view of religious faith, not this book's language, that can benefit from some challenge and change.

God is everywhere. I'm fond of the mystics who remind us that the wall between what is "holy" and what is "earthly" has been broken down in Jesus—God in the flesh, resurrected in the flesh, and present in all creation, not so much to bless that creation as to help us see the blessedness of this earth and of each of us.

So, when you are shopping, when you are eating, when you are playing, when you are arguing, when you are traveling, when you are making love, when you are doing laundry, when you are cooking, cleaning, moving, staying put . . . God is there. When you are looking at each other, like Jacob and Esau, those intensely trying twins in Genesis, you are seeing the face of God.

Is "religious" language wrong? Of course not! God is there, praised there, thanked there, recognized there, and commonly perceived there. But the wise people who included this little book in Holy Scripture have helped us to know that God delights in the human creature and in the joy they—no, in the joy *you* find in each other.

But you don't have to act "religious" (whatever that might mean) to celebrate the goodness of a God who is and defines love. You don't have to mention God in every sentence of prayer or life for God to be not only listening in, but also participating in what is going on. God isn't mentioned in this book, but yes, God is there!

You brought your own religious backgrounds, your own spirituality, your own pilgrimages into your relationship— although you may not have thought of them as that—but you also are in the process of forming your spirituality and pilgrimage as a couple. The lovers in Song of Songs are doing the same and invite you to see God hidden in all of your daily life.

## Some Things to Talk About

1. Did you have a religious element in your upbringing? If so, tell each other what it was like.
2. Have your spirituality and religious life changed over time? Share the experience with each other.
3. What is the most "worldly" activity you each do? Whatever it is, say aloud, "When I ____, God is there." Talk about how saying that made you feel.

## Some Things to Do

1. Drive or walk for half an hour; the route isn't important. After half an hour, stop, rest, and look for God wherever you are. Write a poem (or song or paragraph) about your observations and read it to each other.
2. Do you have a place where it is easier for you to "see" God? Plan to go there together in the coming month.
3. Both of you reveal God to each other. Write a letter to God telling God how that happens. Deliver it to your partner on your partner's birthday.

## Prayer

Holy God, you are a great mystery, and you show your holiness so often by refusing to be distant. You are always creating the earthy stuff of this world. You come to us in water, bread, and wine, in words spoken by a brother or sister, and in the flesh and blood of Jesus. You come to us, amazingly, in and through each other. Thank you for allowing our love to be part of your love. In Christ. Amen.

## There Is a Moment

There is a moment
just as flesh touches flesh
and before two begin
to lose themselves in one.
There is a moment
when all things are suspended
like a comet over dark green trees.
There is a moment
before one moves
and another moves
like a breath about to be taken
or a sigh about to be heard
or the sound of a firefly in a mown field.
There is a moment
when the earth should stop
and think of what will be,
like eyes looking into eyes.

And in that moment
God stops . . . and looks . . .
and smiles . . . and takes joy
in what will happen next.
There is a moment.

# When Hard Times Come

*I opened to my beloved,*
  *but my beloved had turned and was gone.*
*My soul failed me when he spoke.*
*I sought him but did not find him;*
  *I called him but he gave no answer.*
*Making their rounds in the city*
  *the sentinels found me;*
*they beat me, they wounded me. . . .*
  —Song of Songs 5:6,7a

"Hard times, hard times, come again no more. . . ." Songwriter Stephen Foster wrote these words more than a century and a half ago. He echoed a theme in human life from the earliest days of humanity: hard times come most often when we don't choose or expect them. They are part of human experience.

Hard times come in many forms—economics, emotions, jobs or lack of jobs, relationships, health concerns, accidents, violence, and all those interruptions in human life that can be painful and destructive.

Very few people reach adulthood without experiencing some sense of difficult times, so both of you undoubtedly had experience dealing with hard times before you made your commitment to each other. And very few couples go very far together before difficulties arise. That's simply part of life, but sometimes those times are especially difficult.

How does one deal with "hard times"? How do you two deal with them?

Denial, as the cliché goes, is not just a river in Egypt. Some are tempted to downplay the seriousness of things. But when hard times come—illness, financial hardship, emotional struggles, natural disasters, violence—perhaps the most important thing you can do is admit, "This is tough." Be honest with yourself and with each other, and treat the hard time with the serious attention it demands and deserves.

Take a breath. Back off and give yourself some physical and emotional time to absorb the figurative or literal blow. You will need to gather your strength because a shock can knock a lot out of you.

Seek and accept help. That is not a sign of weakness, but of community. Seek friends, seek advice, seek a shoulder to cry on. You don't need to face a difficulty alone. There are pastors; there are counselors; there are people who know what it is to face a particular disease, a particular act of injustice or violence. Seek them out and share all you can with them.

Make a plan. Once you have absorbed the initial blow and taken stock of what you have available in terms of resources, make a plan of steps to deal with the current new reality and work your way back to where you want to be.

Be willing to change your plans. Adjust. If one strategy isn't working, again, pursue other options and make a shift.

In all this, know that you two will become resources and guides for others as well. Resist the temptation to downplay the difficulty others are experiencing; don't rush in too quickly and say, "You'll be okay." Rather, say, "How can I help?" and then offer the assistance you can. Be an ear, give advice if you have it, be a shoulder to cry on and a loving presence. Hard times are not a permanent condition; we move through life, we change, we grow, and we adjust. You have each other to help with that; you have other people who can help you and whom you can help. Hard times will certainly come again, but they can be handled.

### Some Things to Talk About

1. Think about a hard time you or your family experienced when you were growing up. Share the story of that event with your partner.
2. Think back on your life together and the hard times you have faced. Choose one of them. Then talk about how you made it through that season—both what worked and what didn't.
3. Was there a time in your life, either as individuals or as a couple, when someone you knew came to you looking for help or advice? If so, talk about what that was like for you.

### Some Things to Do

1. Plan ahead for crisis. Who are the people you know— friends, family, clergy, counselors—from whom you would seek help and support in a crisis? Make a list of names and contact information.
2. Who has helped you through difficult times in the past? Write a letter to thank those individuals.
3. What organizations in your community help people who are facing difficulties of a kind you are more aware or interested in? Research and agree on ways you can support such organizations.

**Prayer**

God of mercy, we would like for life to never have pain or crises or difficulties, but we know that isn't how life works. You know yourself the pain of rejection, violence, and death, so you feel those things with us, and you also assure us of your love and presence. Help us when we have hard times to continue to love you and love each other. We ask this in your gracious name. Amen.

# Oremus

*Maybe from the beginning*
*the issue was how to live*
*in a world so extravagant*
*it had a sky,*
*in bodies so breakable*
*we had to pray.*
—Stephen Dunn[1]

Let the morning stars reflect the sun,
partners, they, of the waning moon,
as I sit in my backyard
enjoying my coffee.
The sky, not yet bright,
but not still dark,
shelters me
like a
quilt.
Let
this day
be for me—

and not just me—
time for gentleness
in a world grown too mean,
and lives made too breakable
to be able to see the sky
as something more than rain and thunder.
Let this body that is still my own
not be afraid of the decline
that comes to every body,
just as night follows day
to show off the stars
that will give way
in morning
to the
sun.
God,
let us
live lives to
never be numb
to extravagance
that can exult or wound.
Let us live without needing
control that lies beyond our grasp
or answers to all this mystery.
Amen.

**Note**

1. "Ars Poetica." Copyright © 1996 by Stephen Dunn, from WHAT
GOES ON: SELECTED AND NEW POEMS 1995–2009 by Stephen Dunn.
Used by permission of W. W. Norton & Company, Inc.

# Celebrate!

*I come to my garden, my sister, my bride;*
  *I gather my myrrh with my spice,*
  *I eat my honeycomb with my honey,*
  *I drink my wine with my milk.*
*Eat, friends, drink,*
  *and be drunk with love.*
  —Song of Songs 5:1

Humans need times of celebration, occasions that are marked as special and specific and merit extra attention and happiness. We have the calendar's celebrations, of course. In the Christian faith, we have the major holy days of Christmas, the Three Days culminating in Easter (Maundy Thursday, Good Friday, Holy Saturday), Pentecost, saints' days, and other commemorations. Europeans mark "name day"—the saint's day associated with their name—with a special meal and speeches.

Then there are the national holidays—Martin Luther King Day, Mother's Day, Memorial Day, Father's Day, the Fourth of July, Labor Day, Veterans' Day, Thanksgiving Day, and so on. These each have their own significance and particular rituals. We also have personal birthdays—milestones such as 16 and getting a driver's license, 18 and having voting rights, 20, 30, 40, 50, 60, 70, and so on. Other life events—births, graduations, weddings, anniversaries, even the passing of a loved one—call for a break in the normal flow of things. These are special days and times for special observation.

If you are early in your relationship, you are probably still figuring out your own take on these celebrations, what you will bring in from your individual experiences and what you will develop as your very own as a couple. If you have been together for some time, you probably have already molded these days into your own ways—with or without realizing that's what you were doing.

But the fact remains that we like to have those times that are marked as different from other times and bring out rituals and, well, parties!

Sometimes these traditions become predictable and even overbearing (Christmas decorations in August? Come on!), and the perceived necessity to make things special can grind down a person or a family.

What to do? Well, you can start by agreeing on which occasions are the ones more worthy of your work and attention. Some of this will have to do with what you have brought into your relationship from your backgrounds and cultures; some will have to do with your own personal styles and preferences. Take time to prioritize.

But let me suggest this: develop your own times of celebration—times to celebrate you! I don't think the people in the biblical text said, "Every year on the third Thursday of June, we will go to the garden, gather myrrh and spices, honey and honeycomb, wine and milk, and eat and drink and be drunk with love."

Rather, it seems the celebration jumped up for them. You may not be that spontaneous, but maybe it would be good to designate one day each month when you take turns planning a special day—a special trip, a special meal, special gifts, a time to be marked as different and more celebratory than other times. You won't be beholden to Black Friday or decorations or the tyranny of external expectations.

You need special times—some are already there for you, but create your own and celebrate!

### Some Things to Talk About

1. What were your childhood families' most important holidays and celebrations? Share your memories.
2. Tell each other what your ideal birthday party would look like.
3. What was the best celebration each of you ever attended? What made it so good?

### Some Things to Do

1. Take turns planning one celebration (of anything!) each month.
2. Make up your own holiday ("one thing we ought to celebrate once a year") and plan your party.
3. Surprise your partner with an unexpected party or celebration!

### Prayer

God of delight and beauty, you have placed us in a world that is full of what is good and worth celebrating. You have brought us together and kept us together in a love that celebrates your love for the world. Give us hearts that seek joy and happiness for ourselves, for each other, and for this whole world. In Jesus' name. Amen.

# Anniversary in Three-Quarters' Time

When I first saw you, your laughter enthralled
And I knew I would look for you more.
There was something about you, something that called.
You were someone I had waited for.

    So dance with me now as we take to the floor
    And we move with the rhythm so fine.
    It is you that I love, it is you I adore
    As we dance to this—your waltz and mine.

You asked me to join you and share in a dance
And I stood and took you in my arms.
We laughed and we talked and by some lovely chance
I danced myself into your charms.

    So dance with me now as we take to the floor
    And we move with a rhythm so fine.
    It is you that I love, it is you I adore
    As we dance to this—your waltz and mine.

On a beautiful day we pledged our hearts
To be with each other 'til death.
Years have gone by, and, by love's own true arts,
You're still as close to me as my breath.

    So dance with me now as we take to the floor
    And we move with a rhythm so fine.
    It is you that I love, it is you I adore
    As we dance to this—your waltz and mine.

## MY BELOVED, MY FRIEND

Through all these years you have lived with me as
My lover, my teacher, my friend.
I long to be near you for all that life has;
My love for you will never end.

    So dance with me always and take to the floor,
    Let us move with a rhythm so fine.
    For all of these years, now for many years more
    We will dance to this—your waltz and mine.

# In-Laws

*I would lead you and bring you*
   *into the house of my mother,*
   *and into the chamber of the one who bore me.*
*I would give you spiced wine to drink,*
   *the juice of my pomegranates.*
   —Song of Songs 8:2

Making a lifelong commitment to another person is considered so important that the occasion has traditionally not involved just the two persons. There usually must be witnesses and an official of church or state to make the arrangement official, and there often is a group of invited friends. Sometimes that involves a big celebration; in some societies that celebration goes on for days. There is eating and drinking and dancing and speeches and toasts and a great time for the whole community.

Such a commitment even more so involves the families of the partners—the "in-laws"!

That truth has provided the grist for many jokes—for some reason, often at the expense of the mother-in-law, who seems not to be a problem in the text from Song of Songs. It is simply a fact that when you make a commitment to the one you love, nearly always you are also extending that commitment to each other's families.

Now, when you consider that the family is where the one you love learned how to be in a family, learned rules both explicit and implicit about how to behave, and learned (by positive or negative example) what it means to be a partner, it makes sense to know and have some level of comfort with that family.

For those of you who are new to your relationship, you may have a sense of being a stranger—a welcome one, but still a stranger—in the family gatherings. No problem there, really; it is just a matter of you and the in-laws getting to know one another. You have the advantage of loving one whom they love. Those who have been together for years may have moved to the point of feeling as much one of the family as those raised in it.

What you also have discovered or will discover is that your beloved's family may have rules and procedures that they take for granted but that your childhood family would not have done. Becky's family, for instance, pours sugar all over the wonderful Norwegian flatbread called *lefse*, while mine ate it the way God *clearly* intended—with only butter. Neither family could think of doing it otherwise.

You will discover or have discovered more significant differences—in role expectations, meal and bedtime behaviors, travel practices, ways to show affection, and so on. None of these rules or traditions are ultimate or universal, but each can create a bit of friction.

So, talk to each other about what it was like to grow up where you grew up. All through your relationship, not just in the first years, these stories will be important and will help you not only to understand each other but to craft your own family unit—whether that involves just the two of you or children for whose future partners you will be "in-laws."

## Some Things to Talk About

1. What was it like to wake up in your childhood household? Pick a few ages (say, 5, 13, 18) and share what you remember of it.
2. What was it like to meet your beloved's family for the first time? What do you remember about that encounter?
3. What are some of the differences you have discovered in "rules" or conduct in your families? Maybe you haven't told each other about them. Talk about them now.

## Some Things to Do

1. Are your in-laws still alive (both parents-in-law and siblings-in-law)? If so, write a note to each, sharing both news and feelings. (Who gets real letters anymore?)
2. If distance allows, plan a get-together with your in-laws.
3. Following up on "Some Things to Talk About" number 2, try your hand at art and draw a cartoon of your first encounter with your in-laws.

## Prayer

God, when we were babes, you put us into families quite apart from our own choosing, and there you blessed us with life. Now we find ourselves as a family that we have chosen. Bless our choice, dear God. Thank you for those who raised us and those who were raised with us. Help us to see your grace accompanying our growing up and our own life as family. In the name of Christ. Amen.

# Photograph: Mother-in-Law as a Four-Year-Old

You squint into the sun
that shadows your face.
Hand holding hand,
you look beyond the camera.

A photographer's assistant
will add blue to the sky,
pink to your dress,
green to the trees

Behind you,
in the colorless dust
of South Dakota.

You look like
your daughters will look,
like your granddaughters
will look.

Your eyes looking
past the camera,
wondering
who will see.

# Time Away

*Come, my beloved,*
*let us go forth into the fields,*
*and lodge in the villages;*
*let us go out early to the vineyards,*
*and see whether the vines have budded,*
*whether the grape blossoms have opened*
*and the pomegranates are in bloom.*
*There I will give you my love.*
—Song of Songs 7:11-12

When I was young my family never had what might be called a "vacation." Dad would take his vacation pay and then work those weeks for the extra money we needed. We didn't take family vacations, but as kids we went to Bible camp, YMCA camp, Boy Scout camp, and Canoe Base, and we had the Mississippi River to swim in and the Wisconsin bluffs to hike and explore.

We had time away. We all need time away from the daily, the regular, and the familiar to be refreshed and ready for a return to the daily, the regular, and the familiar—as individuals but also as a family.

You may have been raised in a family for whom regular vacations were part of the rhythm. Good for you because, most likely, you have brought that expectation into your adult relationship, and I hope you have made that a part of your lives together.

Vacations don't need to cost a lot—don't let some of the vacation industry fool you into thinking that. Can you camp? Then camp—see whether the grape blossoms have opened and the pomegranates are in bloom. Can you take time away from your regular tasks, a week or two or more, and spend it doing something different, such as day trips, visits around the community, going places you would not otherwise have gone? Most people are surprised by the variety to be found within a short distance.

Can you afford a wider vacation? Some of you have the wherewithal to do so. Others do not, but if that is something you really want, save up for it, plan for it, and make a strategy that cuts expenses and expands opportunities. Maybe your religious group has opportunities for family camps or mission trips. Take advantage of them.

Is one of you a details person? Great, do the details; check the travel deals, the train and bus schedules, and the packages that allow flexibility. Are neither of you details people? Well, buckle up your sense of humor and prepare for an adventure.

Europeans are ahead of us in the United States in that, in some places, vacations are actually required since workers and families return refreshed and ready to enjoy the daily activities, including work. We don't do that here, but, hey, you need time away—as a couple and as a larger family. Give yourselves that necessary gift.

## Some Things to Talk About

1. Did you take vacations or have some kind of time away with family when you were children? Tell each other about those times.

2. If cost were no problem, where would you like to go and what would you like to do? Dream and share with each other.
3. Talk about and develop a bucket list of vacation destinations.

## Some Things to Do

1. Is something in "Some Things to Talk About" number 3 desirable and possible for both of you? Then pick it and begin planning. Assign tasks, discuss them regularly, and share progress reports.
2. Do you have friends with whom a vacation trip would be fun? Contact them and discuss possibilities.
3. Did you not take a honeymoon? It is never too late. Plan one now—or take a second one!

## Prayer

God of work and rest, God of creation and Sabbath, thank you for our daily tasks and thank you for the gift of getting away from those tasks. Give us vision and imagination that we might have time away that delights and refreshes. Thank you for a world of such variety that we are allowed to see and experience. In Jesus' name. Amen.

# The Gunflint Trail

You turn up the trail,
our new canoe an arrow
pointing the way to follow
as we go higher up the hill.
    Red pines next to the road,
    signs of each lake,

    promises of lakes to come,
    promises of years to come.

I turn up the trail;
our dog sleeps in the back seat
dreaming of her loon howl
and steak bones from the landlords.
    Leash leading on portage path,
    diving off granite perch,
    cold water clarifying,
    seeing you among the birch.

We turn up the trail,
our daughters looking out the windows,
cabins, canoes, and woven wool,
a heart-shaped rock retrieved from Canada.
    Daughters laughing around campfire
    canoeing with me to the next lake.
    They sleep in their cabin,
    we watch the stars.

We return up the trail,
our old canoe firmly on the van,
permit purchased in Grand Marais.
Our first canoe alone in decades.
    A stairway to a clear rose lake,
    we scurry to a better site.
    Loons dance on the water;
    we toast them with good red wine.

# You Are a Family

*The mandrakes give forth fragrance,*
    *and over our doors are all choice fruits,*
*new as well as old,*
    *which I have laid up for you, O my beloved.*
    —Song of Songs 7:13

I have to confess that I had some difficulty finding a verse for this meditation. I knew that dealing with "family" is important for couples, but what could I choose—the brothers complaining about a sister's work habits (1:6) or about her physical appearance (8:8)?

But then the verse above came to sight and I thought, well, yes, a family is the existence of "choice fruits, new as well as old. . . ." This can make sense concerning the families in which you were raised and the families that committed couples become, whether they include children or not, whether they are gay or straight, newly born or creatively nurtured in "blended" or adoptive families.

Families nurture. In excellent families, the fruit is always fresh and delicious and always nutritious. But for most of us, families have had some fruit that either is too green or beyond prime, and we try to learn to deal with it. The thing is, like a good fruit salad or a delicious meal, families rarely, if ever, happen just by being thrown together. Rather, they are thought out, directed, and given proper and loving attention.

What are some of the choice fruit that go into being a family?

*Don't hide your emotions;* they make you human and humane. Be able to talk to each other about how you're feeling with words that can express a variety of feelings.

*Laugh together.* Watch funny movies, tell jokes, be able to laugh at your mistakes. *Cry together.* There are things that make us sad—in the world, in our community, in our lives. Tears are cleansing and necessary.

*Play together.* Get some board games, get some active games—Frisbees or balls of various kinds for you to hit, throw, kick, or roll. *Work together*—on projects such as house painting, yard maintenance, holiday planning and decorations.

*Share chores.* Is one of you "the cook"? If that person can share the kitchen, let the other one have a chance, or prepare meals together. Is one of you "the cleaner"? Uh-oh . . . let the other one step in and do a part in that too. It may not be as fun as a movie, but it's nice to get it done.

*Surprise each other with little rewards and gifts.* These don't have to be bought; in fact, those things you make yourself are more special—a letter or card (handwritten and posted!), a poem, a piece of music, a drawing or painting all share something of yourself.

*Go to events*—high school sporting events or theater productions, community events or concerts, parades, speeches, or whatever else is going on in the area. Much of it may be free or at a nominal cost. Talk about what you liked about it and whether you saw something new.

*Talk* . . . to each other . . . a lot.

*Love each other.* Love is not simply being "nice." To love each other means to appreciate who your lover is in old and new "fruit," to hold each other accountable and be able both to challenge and forgive in a genuine and nonaggressive way.

For some families, *having a family theme* for the week, the month, or the year works as a way to focus and provide a touchstone for self-evaluation—to ask questions such as, "How have we grown?" "What have we overcome together?" "Where are we struggling?" "In what ways do we need to grow further?"

You are a family; you may be young or old, gay or straight, just the two of you or a household of generations. In most ways you control how your family lives and grows. You can do it well.

## Some Things to Talk About

1. Each of you write your definition of "family." Share those definitions and discuss how they apply to your family.
2. Is there a family in your circle of friends that you admire? Talk about what you find positive about that family.
3. What are the "fresh fruit"—the good and delicious aspects—of your family?

## Some Things to Do

1. Is someone in the family the regular cook or primary cleaner? Let someone else give a coupon worth a certain number of times to cook, clean, or do some other chore.
2. Discuss some family themes that make sense for your situation then select a theme for the month. Pick a theme that allows you to say, "I did ___ today; it fits our theme because ___."
3. Have a joke night. Give a week in advance to find jokes, puns, or stories you think are good to share for a laugh.

**Prayer**

Holy Trinity, you exist as community, family, unity in diversity. You bring all creation into community of one kind or another. You have brought us together to be a family. Bless this little community, dear God. Help us to love, serve, and appreciate each other. We ask this in your name. Amen.

# For Hudson Robert Schmid
*Born January 18, 2013, at 5:38 a.m.*

(The following poem is a bit long. It is a form called a sestina, and I wrote it for the birth of my brother's grandson.)

Your mother looks through the window at January trees
and at you, as you enjoy your first meal.
Just now, your cries are angel song
for those who waited for you alone—
to birth you and live together,
enjoying life to its distant end.
    Then what do you have at day's end?
    Chip-chirp of cardinals and chickadees in trees,
    the sound of your family gathered together
    eating a hurried meal.
    For now, your universe is you alone;
    soon enough you will choir the song.
Did your grandfather sing you a song?
I see his smile—music that will not end.
He holds you, looks at you alone,
not hearing the rain in the trees
nor planning how to cook the next big meal
when his whole family gets together.

And your grandmother, finally together
with you, holds you, swaddled, like Jesus in the song.
You will see the picture at some birthday meal
and, because you might be "that" age, wish the stories
    to end.
But life's roots pull up ancient water to give its trees
    the urge to grow, to spread and choose not to be alone.
We are born into families, great-nephew, meant not to
    be alone
though at times it is a trial to be together.
When you begin to walk, go with your parents through
    the trees
of southern Minnesota. Learn each bird's song
and look up at a summer sky that will never end
and know that life on earth is a shared meal.
    One day I will sit with you at a family meal
    prepared by Granddad, but now I'm here alone
    rejoicing that our hope has come to this good end;
    grateful, seeing photos of you together
    with your family as moving as a Grieg[1] song,
    lovely as the sight of northern trees.
May you grow to climb trees, savor many a meal,
sing a song that might be heard by you alone,
find joy in each "together," each beginning, each end.

### Note

    1. Edvard Grieg was a noted Norwegian pianist, honored among the
most respected classical composers of the Romantic era.

# Arguing Well, Resolving Graciously

*Catch us the foxes,*
  *the little foxes,*
*that ruin the vineyards—*
  *for our vineyards are in blossom.*
  —Song of Songs 2:15

I remember as a young boy hearing my Great Uncle Will tell an older brother of mine that he looked forward to arguments with Aunt Mary. He didn't like the arguments, he said, but really enjoyed the making up.

Well, old Uncle Will may not have had the best approach to things, but I'm convinced that if two people love each other, they will argue or at least have disagreements that need resolution—because both partners are deeply invested in the relationship. Arguing—that is, arguing well and fairly—is a sign of a strengthening relationship, not a weakening one. Like most things that are worth the effort, arguing well requires practice and work, but the rewards—a deeper trust and more solid relationship—are well worth it.

As is the case with most things, it is best to prepare ahead of time.

Be honest about your emotions. They are necessary but often tricky realities! So, develop a vocabulary of emotions that goes beyond "happy" and "ticked off" because accurately described emotions are key to resolving conflict. Also remember that anger is considered a "secondary emotion." That is, it comes from another emotion—fear, surprise, or hurt, for instance. So, take time to unearth what your primary emotion might be.

Be fair with each other. Part of that entails communicating in "I" messages. Instead of saying, "You infuriate me when you leave clothes on the bedroom floor for days!" you might say, "I feel frustrated when dirty clothes are left on the bedroom floor."

Another part of playing fair is establishing that either of you can "call a conference" to discuss an issue. Only one person need ask, and whenever that happens, the other one will agree to the discussion. Set time aside—specific time—to discuss what can be done.

It may not sound very romantic, but in some ways a marriage is like a corporate merger. "Calling a conference" is essentially a request for negotiation—and the first step in any negotiation is identifying what the issue is. Note that the issue is not framed as an accusation (not, for example, "You think I'm a pig" or "You think I'm too picky," but "There are dirty clothes on the bedroom floor").

Having agreed on the issue, discuss options for resolution. If something hasn't worked in the past, it won't work in the future. Agree on specific things for each of you to do (write them down), and then schedule another meeting later to evaluate how you've done. And keep in mind that resolution shouldn't be a personal victory (or loss) for either partner.

Assuming that you use these strategies effectively—that you treat each other fairly, you're honest about your emotions, and you both are dedicated to finding a resolution that doesn't involve a winner or a loser—you should see most contentions resolved without third-party mediation!

Now celebrate.

Thank each other for the hard work involved, talk about what you've learned about your relationship and your individual gifts, and store those things away in your hearts for future reference. The honesty of the argument is matched by the graciousness of the resolution.

## Some Things to Talk About

1. Experiment with "I" messages. State the same issue first as a "You made me" claim, and then as an "I am" statement. (It's probably best to try this first outside the context of a disagreement.) Discuss the differences between the two approaches.
2. Has one of you "called a conference" to discuss an issue? Did the other partner agree? Take time to discuss your feelings about that experience.
3. At some point a disagreement will arise. Deal with it well and graciously; when it is over, talk about how you both felt about the process.

## Some Things to Do

1. Work on a list of emotion words; be creative and as complete as possible. (Need help? You can find playful, graphic representations of a wide variety of emotions online by searching "How Are You Feeling Today?")
2. Do you have friends who seem to handle disagreements and arguments well? If you think they would be okay with this, ask them what their strategy is.
3. If you are careful planners, draw up a list of disagreement topics and rate the level of energy they're worth, from 5 (least worthy) to 1 (most worthy).

## Prayer

Dear God, you know a bit about arguments, disagreements, and hurt feelings. Yet your will has been to seek restoration of what is good. Thank you for making us people who can feel, react, and resolve. Forgive us for those times we have not listened well to each other. Thank you for those times when we have. Give us love, grace, and graciousness toward each other. We ask this in Jesus' name. Amen.

# Silas Goes to Bed

Why should the simplest of human actions
    be simple?
        You teach me that complications
            enrich.
            Rather than marching upstairs you race
            around the house;
    the act of taking a bath
is Olympic.

Putting on pajamas could take seconds
    or hours,
        and the debate over which lights stay on:
            Gladstone/Disraeli.*
            Anyone, you teach, can be quiet, still, tired
            then fall asleep,
    but your extra effort wrestles fatigue
and wins.

I know you are close to sleep when shouts
    become tears;
        long after my own weariness,
            you sleep.
            In the morning I see you still, peaceful,
            pretzel-splayed.
    I stand by your door, watch your slumber,
and love you.

* British prime ministers during Queen Victoria's reign, known
  for their bitter rivalry.

# Money

*If one offered for love*
    *all the wealth of one's house,*
    *it would be utterly scorned.*
    —Song of Songs 8:7b

As the Beatles sang: "Money can't buy me love." That is certainly true. But we know that living in an economy such as ours, money can buy food, clothing, transportation, housing, and so on. Love cannot be bought with money, but a relationship can get pretty messed up by it.

My mother met my father when they were both young and working at Erickson's Bakery in LaCrosse, Wisconsin. Mom said she was drawn to Dad by the way he kneaded dough. "We got married and we've been needing dough ever since," said my pun-loving mom. That "needing" is a challenge when it happens and it can strain a relationship.

If you've been together for a while, you have had some experience—some positive, some negative—dealing with your finances. If you are newly together, you may or may not have a well-defined plan for handling your money. If you're somewhere between these two, you also have a sense of what the realities of finance has meant, means now, and will mean in your relationship.

Depending on where you are in your life journey, your concerns, perspectives, and experiences related to finances will differ, but in those differences, these guidelines all apply: be knowledgeable, be realistic, be disciplined, be gracious, and have a plan.

Be knowledgeable. Even if just one of you is the "chief financial officer" of the family, both partners need to know what resources and income you have available and what the expenses will be. It is a good idea to sit down with some regularity and look at your finances together. If you have a budget, see how closely you are following it; if you don't have a budget, create one. Really, it will make life easier.

Be realistic and be disciplined. Once you have a fairly accurate sense of income and expenses, try very hard to stay close to your expectations. Be disciplined when you have to put off some purchases and scale back some desires. Be disciplined when you have extra resources available but have already planned how to, shall we say, expand your purchase power! If you're just starting out, establish a savings account of some type. Think of yourselves—your present and future as a couple—as one of the monthly bills you have to pay.

Be gracious. Money is not simply "filthy lucre," but part of God's creation.[1] It is one way that we live in and for the world. Things may not work as you budgeted and disciplined for, and that often causes tension in a relationship. Take a breath, back away (at least emotionally), and make a point of enjoying each other. Or perhaps things work out much better than you budgeted or planned. Rejoice, give thanks, and make a point of enjoying each other.

Have a plan—a plan for the current week and month, a plan for the coming years, a plan for retirement—have a plan. If you have life insurance (and you really should), your agent is probably a Certified Financial Planner™ (CFP®) and will be able to help you, often for free (well, not free, really, but as a benefit with your paid premiums). The CFP® will be able to help with plans appropriate for your stage in life and in relationship.

Money may be a source of stress but when you gain a sense of control, you can make it your servant.

## Some Things to Talk About

1. If you had all the money you needed, what would you do with it? Think about it and discuss your ideas together.
2. What has been your greatest concern about money so far in your relationship? What has been your greatest satisfaction about money so far?
3. What do you remember about your parents and money when you were a child? Compare notes.

## Some Things to Do

1. Do you have a budget? If so, do you review it regularly to assess actual versus budgeted figures—and to update it as circumstances of income and expense change? If so, good for you; if not (on any point), take time to develop a realistic budget and then schedule regular reviews.
2. Make a list of your financial goals for one year, five years, and ten years from now. Then discuss ways to achieve these goals—perhaps with your CFP®.
3. Do you share your money with others via charitable giving (such as to your local faith community or a favorite nonprofit)? Why or why not? Discuss why such giving is a good idea, and if you aren't already giving, pick a good organization to support financially.

**Prayer**

God of immense wealth and immense generosity, we know that all we have comes from you and we don't always thank you. Thank you, God, for what we have. Give us hearts that are glad and generous as well. See us safely through times of financial insecurity and help us to rejoice in those times of plenty. We ask this in Jesus' name. Amen.

# Treasures
*for Matt and Angie*

In twenty-five years
will they value time spent
in my office
more than the walk they took
to get here?
I hope not!
My prayer for them:
May they still treasure each other
over other treasures.
May their first walk to Picnic Point,
their walk down a short aisle,
walks through schools,
degrees, job offers and so on
until they can no longer walk
be blessed by their company
more than by their surroundings.

As their smiles age,
may they grow
into each other's laughter,
may they sigh and walk,
cry and forgive,
and live life as they live now—
alive in the treasure
of joyful, growing love.

## Note

1. Judson Press has published a great resource related to the biblical purposes of money—spending, saving, giving, and investing—and how each person is more naturally disposed toward one use or another. *Money on Purpose: Finding a Faith-Filled Balance* by Shayna Lear, a Certified Financial Planner™ who holds both an MDiv and MBA, offers the reader help in identifying one's own "financial personality"—and how your personality might relate to your partner's! Order online at www.judsonpress.com or by calling 800-4-JUDSON.

# Scary Love?

*You are beautiful, my love, as Tirzah,*
*majestic as Jerusalem,*
*daunting*
*as stars in their courses.*
*Your eyes! Turn them away*
*for they dazzle me.*
    —Song of Songs 6:4-5, Bloch

Do you remember your first date? Oh, not your first date with each other (unless that was your first date ever), but your very first date . . . do you remember it? How relaxed and calm were you then? Unless you are one of the few, you were anything but relaxed or calm.

Something about the attraction we feel for another human being, a desire that God has planted in us, touches what is holy. And the holy inspires awe—which is another word for fear. In the Bible, unlike in modern TV shows, whenever people encountered God or God's angels, they were scared—*really* scared! Not all fear is good or holy; some is the result of things that are bad and harmful. But there is a fear, a terror, an awe, a refusing-to-be-at-ease about love—when it is love—that is like the holy fear experienced in the presence of God or the angels.

In the Song of Songs the woman expresses awe; she says, "Do not stir up or awaken love until it is ready!" (2:7, and repeated twice more). The man expresses *fear*. He seems to realize that real manliness in love is never simply being *macho*. It means being vulnerable and "weak" enough to be loved. The apostle Paul agreed when he said that only when he is weak can he be strong (2 Corinthians 12:10).

Beauty is not just flowers in a meadow or soft music or aromatherapy. Beauty can have the same impact as seeing the banners of a victorious army coming closer and closer and closer, as the NRSV translates the second half of verse 4—*terrible as an army with banners*—a heart-in-your-throat kind of feeling. Beauty can have the same impact as seeing a thunderstorm moving across the sky in your direction, or looking up at the Milky Way on a clear night in the wilderness. Beauty can have the same impact as the terrified, suspenseful waiting for the arrival of a new child.

Love is scary because love reflects the holy. Love is terrifying—awe-inspiring and breathtaking—in its own way because love makes us vulnerable. Love means entering a new reality, not simply stopping by for a visit. Love is daunting and dazzling.

The man in the Song is scared, but he doesn't run—at least he doesn't run *away*. Rather he runs into her arms. The woman is in awe of the power of love, but she does not keep her distance. Rather, deciding the time is now, she steels her heart and leans into love with all its risks and uncertainties; she goes, seeks, and pursues her beloved. Any love worth the name is "terrible as an army with banners."

## Some Things to Talk About

1. Talk to each other about your first dating experience (assuming it wasn't with each other!). How did it feel? How did it go?
2. What was your first date together like? Who asked whom? How did it feel—asking or being asked, getting ready, going out? Go on another date and compare the two experiences.
3. Recall images of beauty and awe that you have seen. Describe them. Which of them might you use to describe the beauty and awe of love . . . of *your* love?

## Some Things to Do

1. Ride together on a roller coaster, a water slide, or some other fun and scary ride.
2. Find a way to escape light pollution on a clear night and watch the stars and night sky together.
3. Next time there is a thunderstorm, turn off the lights in your home and experience the storm holding hands.

## Prayer

God of awe and beauty, so much in this world is both awesome and beautiful, both terrible and lovely. There is so much that we see and don't know whether to run to it or run away from it. Dear God, sometimes even the love we have for each other is so strong it is scary. Other times it seems so weak that we are frightened. But always you have blessed our love and helped us to share it. Continue to be with us to bless and keep us in loving awe. In Jesus' name. Amen.

# Franklin Avenue

Walking up to Market Fair,
I pass the corner.
If I turn right, I will see you
when you come home from work.
I want to sit on your front steps,
listen to the sounds of muffled city,
watch people passing by, and
smile at you as you walk up the street.
I want to hold out my hands to you,
feel your hands in mine,
look into your eyes, kiss you,
and hold you close.
I would feel you breathing,
your head leaning on my shoulder,
our arms around each other,
and the world passing us by.
I think of this as I cross the street.
I think of this as I go through the aisles.
I pay for groceries and walk home,
thinking . . . "She lives up there!"

# Take Care of Yourself

*My vineyard is all my own.*
*Keep your thousand, Solomon! And pay*
*two hundred to those*
*who must guard the fruit.*
  —Song of Songs 8:12, Bloch

When you made a life commitment to each other, each of you promised (with one phrase or another) to care for the other through all manner of possibilities. That is a lifelong commitment and a sign of the love and respect you have for each other. Good for you!

There is another person in the couple who also deserves love and respect—and that is you!

In a way that makes great sense. How can you care for another if you do not take care of yourself? How can you "love another as you love yourself" if you don't, in fact, love yourself? Now, we're not talking about an all-consuming self-centeredness or an unconcerned, uninvolved selfishness. We're talking about stewardship of God's gifts—the gift of your beloved and the gift that is you yourself.

You care deeply about each other. Because that is true, you can care very deeply about yourself, your needs, your health—mentally, physically, spiritually—your requirements for rest, for variety, and for self-care. Your "vineyard" may not be the grandest in the land, but it is yours and your care for it makes it beautiful and productive.

How do you exercise self-care? You do so first by being careful about yourself. And you're fortunate because the two of you have an in-house coach—each other. You don't have to be fanatic and nit-picking for yourself or your partner; just show love by exercising some common sense.

Pay attention to nutrition—what you buy and what you eat. Charts for healthy eating are all around you; you can't fail to see them. Eat fruits and vegetables; watch the red meat intake; get your fiber and your fluids. Be moderate in your choice of what and how much to drink (for example, alcohol, caffeine, sugar, artificial sweeteners). Help each other out—there's lots of healthy food out there that is also tasty!

Don't smoke.

Get plenty of rest.

Exercise. You could join a gym, but you don't need to. Walk or hike; ride a bike; swim or canoe; get into the woods and wilderness with some regularity.

Pray, meditate, and pay attention to your inner life. Prayer and meditation don't involve sitting at the feet of a guru for decades. You talk to each other; talk to God too. Meditate. Seek somewhere quiet; get relaxed; close your eyes; feel your breath move in and out; find a phrase or Bible verse that means a lot to you and run it through your mind.

Keep a journal of your thoughts, your hopes, your dreams (your literal, sleeping dreams and your figurative dreams and hopes). Share them with each other.

Learn how to forgive. Studies in forgiveness at the University of Wisconsin–Madison have shown that forgiveness is immensely beneficial to the one who forgives. Grudges weigh you down.

Get regular physicals and dental checkups. Pay attention to the advice and directions you receive there.

And remember, the better you take care of yourself, the better you take care of your partner.

## Some Things to Talk About

1. When do you feel best about your whole self? When don't you feel so good about your whole self? Talk to each other about both experiences, and identify any patterns.
2. What were your earliest experiences in a doctor's or dentist's office? Discuss how those experiences may have influenced your attitudes and habits about physical and dental health.
3. Talk to each other about what you enjoy most—and least—about physical exercise.

## Some Things to Do

1. Develop a nutrition and exercise plan (if you don't already have one). Do research, perhaps visit a nutritionist or personal trainer, and make plans that you will both enjoy and stick with. Keep each other encouraged.
2. Do you take time for prayer and meditation? If not, agree on a time for both of you to be in silence, meditation, and prayer. After that, take time to share your perceptions with each other.
3. Do you have a primary care physician? Do you have a dentist? Do you have health insurance? If the answer to any of these questions is no, act so that it becomes a yes.

**Prayer**

God of ongoing creation, we know you not only gave us our bodies and minds, but you are even now still giving them, blessing them, and being present in them. Give us the grace to be good caretakers of ourselves. Give us the grace to be kind in encouraging each other's self-care, and always help us to have awe and appreciation for the lives we have. In Christ. Amen.

# For Silas on His Eighth Birthday

Two hopes (or prayers) I have for you today.
May unread years that lie ahead of you
Be good books you will open up with joy
As you grow. Sit beside me, grandson,
Today we will move on—you and I—
And spend our time the best of ways,
No sitting serious at a frowning desk—
They will always be there waiting. Let
Them wait. You are now eight years old!
And patiently, you've counted down the hours
A passage for this January day
And gave me a brief time to be your friend.
You are, grandson, a reader of not just books
But of dreams and hopes to keep inside;
When the time is right you'll open, spread
Beauty on your world with all of them.
Think, Silas, what the world will be for you
Then. And now hear my second hope (or prayer):
May you search and may that quest not be
Easy but may it make you a good man.

# Growing Old

*O my dove, in the clefts of the rock,*
*in the covert of the cliff,*
*let me see your face,*
*let me hear your voice;*
*for your voice is sweet*
*and your face is lovely.*
  —Song of Songs 2:14

Young love is, well, *young* love, and it has all its own beauty and strength and focus and attention. Every couple reading these lines has experienced young love. Some people reading these lines are experiencing the beauty, strength, focus, and attention that are part of love for all who are growing old.

The verb *growing* is important. To move forward and into advanced years is not a decline but a growth. That's important to know, living, as we still do, in a culture that glorifies youth and, at best, ignores or trivializes old age.

A Finnish saying points out, "Old age comes, but it doesn't come alone." Every age has not only its beauty, strength, focus, and attention but its challenges as well. As we grow into each age, we move into its challenges. And growth into our senior years certainly presents challenges—health changes, physical changes, vocational and lifestyle changes. Greet them.

I have been privileged to live with Becky for more than four decades, and I still see her face, hear her voice, and celebrate her loveliness because they and I have grown into our sixties with her. If you are a couple who have shared decades together, think of that growth and the movement into what the poet Robert Browning described as "the last of life, for which the first was made"[1] and celebrate that growth.

That doesn't mean the challenges disappear—no more than the challenges of infancy, adolescence, youth, young adulthood, or middle age disappear when each age is celebrated. Sometimes that growth involves more challenges than you would have chosen. Don't minimize or ignore them; such challenges are real and you overcome them only by facing them. You face them well by facing them together.

As part of a couple, when you grow into that new age, you will have a partner with you. Your partner, if he or she is a contemporary, will also be experiencing similar growth. You are there for each other. Share the joys and the challenges of this new age. Find ways to celebrate the joys and other ways to confront the challenges.

In the book of Job, near the end, God addresses Job from a whirlwind. A commentator on that text has noted that often it is not so much the words, but the presence of the one who shares them that is healing.

You have already grown into old age—or you will grow into it soon enough. Seek ways to be grateful for that growth and to be grateful for the beloved friend who grows into that age along with you.

## Some Things to Talk About

1. If you are young and new in your partnership together, reflect aloud on what growth into old age may be like. If you have shared many years together, take time to talk about the highlights of that growth.
2. Whatever the years of your partnership, give some thought to the joys and challenges you remember from each "age" through which you have passed as individuals and as a couple—childhood, adolescence, young adulthood, middle age, advanced age. Share those insights together.
3. Younger couples, finish this sentence: "When we grow older, our love will be. . . ." Older couples, finish these sentences: "Our young love was like our love now in these ways. . . . It is different from our love now in these ways. . . ."

## Some Things to Do

1. Whose growth into old age has made an impression on you? If the two of you and that person are comfortable with it, arrange a get-together to express your appreciation and seek suggestions.
2. If you are a younger couple, identify an older couple whose friendship you would value. Reach out to them. If you are an older couple, seek a younger couple whose friendship you would value, and reach out to them.
3. Watch a movie together about love and friendship in advanced years (such as *On Golden Pond*, *The Best Exotic Marigold Hotel*, or *Quartet*).

**Prayer**

God of childbirth and growth through the ages, you bless all
life through every stage. Thank you for where we are now in
our lives. Give us vision to rejoice in the joys we have and
grace to deal with the challenges. Bless our growing into each
new chapter of life; help us to hold each other as you hold us.
In your name. Amen.

# Sometimes Seventeen Minutes

He never thought much about rain
or, when rains came, seeking shelter
when he was young—only seventeen,
and hours meant as much as minutes.
He could as easily take the school bus
or choose to return home in a quick walk.

So he would take a wet walk,
enjoying the moist touch of rain,
watch his friends pass on the bus
and never think that home was a shelter
to which he would return in minutes
at the age of seventeen.

But when his youngest was seventeen,
he found he would rather ride than walk
because time is money and profits cost minutes.
He did not enjoy the sound or feel of rain;
when it began, he looked for shelter
but would never ride a bus.

He went to college on a bus,
a freshman at the age of seventeen
with an intellect that provided shelter
and thoughts to consider on his walk
across the small town campus in autumn rain,
a walk he could finish in minutes.

Now, seventy, retired, and minutes
away from all he needs by bus,
he looks out the window and watches the rain.
He will meet friends, spend seventeen
dollars on beer and steak, and walk
in post-rain humidity to apartment's shelter.

He thinks of things that shelter,
and the ceaseless sifting of minutes,
looking ahead to an evening walk
to meet his wife, arriving by bus,
soon, at nine-seventeen.
They will hold hands and listen to the rain.

Rain helps us love a shelter but
sometimes seventeen minutes with one we love is enough—
better transport than a bus, more grounded than a walk.

**Note**

1. From Robert Browning, "Rabbi Ben Ezra," line 3.

# Love and Death

*Set me as a seal upon your heart,*
*   as a seal upon your arm;*
*for love is as strong as death,*
*   passion as fierce as the grave.*
   —Song of Songs 8:6

Folk singer Jim Post wrote a song about the death of his grandfather. "Three Soft Touches" describes the scene in the hospital room as his grandmother sits next to his dying grandfather. Before he dies, the grandfather reaches out and gently taps three times on his wife's hand.

During breakfast the next morning, Grandmother tells the family that when they were dating, Grandfather would tap her three times to say "I love you." He did that so he could speak his heart to her in words only she would "hear." He had done that again before he died, she said, and the touch brought back all those years they had shared together.

We will die. That is not a morbid or depressing sentence: it simply states the nature of things on this earth.

We can let the reality of death float over us like a dark cloud. We can let it keep us from ever enjoying anything. Just as easily, we can let the reality of death be a spice that makes each day special and important. We can do that as Christians because we are told that Christ has defeated death's hold on us. "Death," as poet Dylan Thomas wrote, "shall have no dominion."[1]

In the ancient world, a seal was the mark of someone of authority. The symbol of a king or governor would be pressed into clay or wax, so that the impression would be deep and the soft substance would quickly harden. To break a physical seal might be punishable by death—because the symbolic seal was unbreakable. Love made that kind of permanent claim on the hearts of the lovers. The passion experienced was as enduring and unyielding as the grave itself—and beyond.

The lovers in the Song of Songs lived life in such a way that they could face Death and say, "Okay, you may be strong, but look at this: our love will outlast you. You will touch us at the end, but we will touch each other and that touch, that love will keep my beloved with me even after you try to separate us all through this life we have."

Some day, one of you and one of us will not be here. But until that day, we live life so that not only the memories but also each day will be blessed and beautiful.

### Some Things to Talk About

1. Talk to each other about what you may fear most about death. What provisions can you make for each other to ease those fears?
2. Talk about your personal preferences for your funeral (place, people, music, care of your body), knowing these things can be changed. Take notes as appropriate so that you can honor each other's requests.
3. Tell each other why you are happy you still have each other. Share what memories you will cherish about each other when one of you should die.

## Some Things to Do

1. Write a letter to your lover, to be read after you have died. Seal the letters and agree on a safe place to store them— perhaps with your last will and testaments.
2. If you haven't already done so, draft a last will and testament. You can find simple forms online or at an office supply store, or you may consult with an attorney. Also consider completing an advance directive (living will) that specifies your wishes related to end-of-life care, do-not-resuscitate orders, and organ donation.
3. Whom do you know whose lifelong partner has died? Mourning decreases but never really ends. Reach out to the survivor to express your love and support.

## Prayer

God of the living and the dead, we don't especially look forward to dying. We ask you to give us long life and years to be together. But we know we will die someday. You know what it is like to enter death. To know that you will be there at the other side of the grave gives us strength. Grant us long life, if that is your will, dear God. But especially give us life that is filled with appreciation for life and great love for each other. In Jesus' name. Amen.

## Note

1. From Thomas's poem by that title.

## Haibun

*\* Haibun is a form of Japanese writing that combines prose and poetry, specifically haiku.*

You are retired and I am soon retired. Your project has been cleaning out the clutter of this house we've inhabited for more than twenty years. You find a lot of junk, of course, but also reminders of where we have been—forgotten photographs of pets and daughters; Leah's middle school identification cards; toys given over scores of Christmases and birthdays; placards, postcards, and pants.

You tell me you have a surprise for me and bring me a cigar box full of letters I had written to you the year before our marriage—on Luther College stationery for crying out loud! I read them. . . . Some make me cry and some leave me laughing out loud. So easy for young people to pledge undying love, and so amazing that love kisses the dying.

Everywhere, beauty—
Old ink, old paper, young love;
Summers birth winters.

# Where To?

*O woman in the garden,*
*all our friends listen for your voice.*
*Let me hear it now.*
*Hurry, my love! Run away,*
*my gazelle, my wild stag*
*on the hills of cinnamon.*
    —Song of Songs 8:13-14, Bloch

The book ends with these two verses. In the first, the man in the story asks to hear the voice of the beloved. In the second, the woman invites the lover into a world of action and freedom. In both verses, and throughout the whole book, there is always an openness to the future. That openness comes not because what is coming is certain and secure, but because the relationship is committed and loving.

Canadian theologian Douglas John Hall has said about the Christian faith, "Confidence we may now and then feel; certitude, never."[1] I believe that applies to committed relationships as well. We approach the future not with *certainty* ("I know exactly what will be") but with *confidence* ("I trust you and will move ahead with you").

As human beings we are more like movies than photographs. We never stay the same; we never stop changing. Our relationships are like that too. Because we are committed in love to each other, we are committed to change—because our loved one doesn't just sit there and remain exactly the same as when we first met. We grow, change, move, and continue. In a strange way, our love for each other makes that movement into the future both easier and more difficult.

It is easier because we have a partner. "It is not good to be alone" is one of God's first observations about the human creature (see Genesis 2:18). We have someone with whom we can share in trust and in intimacy.

Movement into the future together is also more difficult because we commit ourselves to the journey and to each other. That commitment requires work, requires trust, requires love that shifts and changes to match the conditions and needs of the beloved.

But that journey is good. It is worth the effort. It is worth the commitment. "Let me hear your voice now. . . ." "Hurry, my love!"

### Some Things to Talk About

1. Share with each other one great hope for your future.
2. Share with each other one concern for your future.
3. The last verse speaks of "hills of cinnamon." If you had to give a spice to the hills of your future, what would it be and why?

### Some Things to Do

1. Go for a walk or a ride through your favorite hills or countryside.
2. Write a letter to each other and have it delivered in one year.
3. Approach the future with confidence; plan a big trip to take place in three to five years and then start working to see it happen.

**Prayer**

God of all times, thank you for holding not only our times, but each of us in your care, concern, and love. We can't be certain of exactly what the future will be for us, but we ask you to give us confidence in you, in each other, and in what lies ahead. Thank you for the past that has brought us here; thank you for the future we are entering. Amen.

## Listening to Ein Heldenleben[2]

In late night quiet we look
   at the old photographs
     on the wall
And we drift out of bed,
   slip into the field, past the prairie,
     past the trees.
We stop there, holding hands,
   gazing over the last hill
     and into each other's eyes.
Our lives lie out there
   beyond the horizon
     into which we walk.

**Notes**

1. Douglas John Hall, *Bound and Free: A Theologian's Journey* (Minneapolis: Augsburg Fortress, 2005), 131.
2. The symphonic piece "Ein Heldenleben" is a tone poem by composer Richard Strauss. Its German title means "A Hero's Life."

# SOME ADVICE FOR
# RETREAT LEADERS

This book is intended primarily as a way to help couples talk to each other, share with each other, continue to learn from each other, and grow their relationship. This also should be a primary aim in a retreat setting, but a retreat allows for an expanded dynamic.

I am a Lutheran and for much of my life I experienced "retreats" simply as a name for moving the classroom from the church basement to a lovely setting nobody gets to see since they are all in class! Fortunately, this is becoming less the norm.

A retreat is a chance to get away from the norm, to take a breath, to engage in thought and meditation, to appreciate relationship with God, with self, and, in this case, with one's significant other at a deeper level. Here are my suggestions to help you lead a valuable retreat.

First, decide on the optimum number of couples you wish to facilitate. No more than a dozen would be best. It would be best to have a diversity of new couples and more seasoned couples and of couples from various races and cultures; if it is appropriate for your community, a mix of both gay and straight couples also would be good.

Then, see that each couple has a copy of the meditation titles before an initial planning gathering. Invite them to identify the topics they would most like covered in the retreat. Ask them also to read the Song of Songs. Each couple should have a copy of this book as the retreat begins. If the retreat is Friday night through Sunday afternoon, as is often the case, I suggest one topic on Friday (most suitably Meditation One), no more than four on Saturday, and one on Sunday (perhaps Meditation Twenty-six).

Familiarize yourself thoroughly with the contents of this book and the contents of the Song of Songs. You would benefit from a good Bible commentary. Your church library or public or university library should have some. I recommend the commentary by Ariel and Chana Bloch (whose translation of the biblical text I also very much like), *The Song of Songs: A New Translation*, University of California Press, 1995.

No less than two weeks before the retreat, meet with the registered participants and come to a consensus on which topics are to be covered. Then you have some work to do as the retreat leader!

Put together any movies, clippings, ads, cartoons, indeed anything from culture that you think would help couples focus. Design simple worship experiences to open and close each day of the retreat. Each session begins in prayer and with just a few summary statements from you about the meditation about to be considered. (For instance, "This first meditation looks at your relationship as a gift and asks you to talk with each other about what you see special about each other. I'm going to show a film clip from the Broadway musical *The Music Man*, where Harold and Marian finally express their love for each other. . . .")

You may want to provide the full biblical text for participants to ensure that a single translation is available for group discussion. I recommend a modern translation such as the New Revised Standard Version or Common English Bible. You might also encourage people to bring their personal Bibles, supply pew Bibles or photocopies of the text, or invite folks to use smartphones or tablets to access a Bible app or website such as BibleGateway.com or StudyLight.org.

Give the participants an hour alone as couples to read the meditation, to think over and discuss the "Some Things to Talk About" section, and perhaps to consider the "Some Things to Do" section. Don't imprison them. If the retreat setting offers a pleasing outdoor setting, release the couples to go for a walk or find a place outside to talk. Just clearly establish a time to reconvene in an agreed-upon location. After an hour, allow fifteen minutes to let participants gather again; have snacks available during that gathering time. Then take half an hour for couples to discuss any insights or questions they may have.

Possible conversation prompts include:

"What did you learn that would be of value for other couples?"

"What questions do you have about this meditation?"

"What should be explored more?"

"What's something about this meditation you wish you had known before?"

"How could the meditation be improved for your use?"

Don't fill every minute. This is a retreat! Allow time to relax, to take walks, to nap, to be unscheduled and at leisure. Here is a possible schedule:

**Friday Evening**

Arrival, room assignments, unpacking

Time for refreshments

Large group meets for introductions—*Ask participants to share their names, hometowns, how long the couple has been together, and what they are looking forward to in this retreat.*

Dramatic reading of the Song of Songs—*Distribute copies; summarize this book's introduction to Song of Songs and then start the reading. Recruit volunteer readers ahead of time, or you and your partner (if you have one) serve as the voices for the book. Invite response from participants.*

Couple discussion time (60 minutes)—*Invite each couple to read and discuss the first chosen meditation on their own.*

Gathering time (15 minutes)

Large group discussion

Worship—*Include prayer and song.*

**Saturday**

Breakfast

9:00—Next meditation and discussion

11:00—Free time

Noon—Lunch

1:00—Next meditation and discussion

3:00—Free time

5:00—Dinner

6:30—Next meditation and discussion

8:00—Fellowship break

8:30—Final meditation and discussion of the day

10:00—Worship

**Sunday**

Breakfast

9:00—Final meditation and discussion

11:00—Free time

11:30—Worship

Noon—Lunch

Afternoon—*Depending on time constraints, time for informal discussion, packing, and returning home.*

Plan and pray; pray and plan. The retreat will be a positive and nurturing experience for all involved.

# FOR FURTHER READING

## Commentaries and Translations

Robert Atler, *Strong As Death Is Love: The Song of Songs, Ruth, Esther, Jonah, and Daniel, A Translation with Commentary*. New York: W.W. Norton and Company, 2015.

Ariel Bloch and Chana Bloch, *The Song of Songs: A New Translation*. Berkeley: University of California Press, 1995.

Carey Ellen Walsh, *Exquisite Desire: Religion, the Erotic and the Song of Songs*. Minneapolis: Augsburg/Fortress, 2000.

## Poetry

Hafiz, *The Subject Tonight Is Love: 60 Wild and Sweet Poems of Hafiz,* Daniel Ladinsky, translator. New York: Penguin Compass, 2003. Any of the works of Hafiz are worth reading.

Kabir, *The Ecstatic Poems,* Robert Bly, translator. Boston: Beacon Press, 2004.

Rumi (Jalāl ad-Dīn Muhammad Rūmī), *The Essential Rumi: New Expanded Edition,* Coleman Barks, translator. San Francisco: Harper Collins, 2007 (or any of several translations by Coleman Barks). Rumi was a Muslim mystic whose love poetry to God has also become popular as poetry suitable between two people. As with Hafiz, any of Rumi's works are good reading!

## Resources for Couples

Harold L. Arnold, *Marriage ROCKS for Christian Couples.* Valley Forge, PA: Judson Press, 2009. Leader's guide also available.

Robert Atwell, *Love: 100 Readings for Marriage.* Louisville: Westminster John Knox, 2005.

Gary D. Chapman, *The Five Love Languages: The Secret to Love That Lasts.* Chicago: Northfield Publishing, 2015.

Carol Erdahl and Lowell O. Erdahl, *Be Good to Each Other: An Open Letter on Marriage.* Minneapolis: Augsburg/Fortress, 1991.

Marvin A. McMickle, *Before We Say I Do: 7 Steps to a Healthy Marriage.* Valley Forge, PA: Judson Press, 2003.

Ella Pearson Mitchell and Henry H. Mitchell, *Together for Good: Lessons from Fifty-Five Years of Marriage.* Valley Forge, PA: Judson Press, 2005.

David H. Olson, Amy K. Olson-Sigg, and Peter J. Larson, *The Couple Checkup.* Minneapolis: Life Innovations Prepare/Enrich, 2008. Available online at www.prepare-enrich.com.